An Introduction *to* **Structured Query Language**

Ron McFadyen
University of Manitoba

Vijay Kanabar
University of Winnipeg

 Wm. C. Brown Publishers

Book Team
Editor *Matt Loeb*
Developmental Editor *Linda Meehan*
Production Coordinator *Carla D. Arnold*

 Wm. C. Brown Publishers
President *G. Franklin Lewis*
Vice President, Publisher *George Wm. Bergquist*
Vice President, Publisher *Thomas E. Doran*
Vice President, Operations and Production *Beverly Kolz*
National Sales Manager *Virginia S. Moffat*
Advertising Manager *Ann M. Knepper*
Marketing Manager *Craig S. Marty*
Editor-in-Chief *Edward G. Jaffe*
Managing Editor, Production *Colleen A. Yonda*
Production Editorial Manager *Julie A. Kennedy*
Production Editorial Manager *Ann Fuerste*
Publishing Services Manager *Karen J. Slaght*
Manager of Visuals and Design *Faye M. Shilling*

Cover design by SHEPHERD

To my wife Susan, and my children Niall and Colin
R.M.

To my wife Dina, son Anish and daughter Meera
V.K.

Contents

Preface

For more than a decade, Structured Query Language (SQL) has competed with several other languages to become the standard for relational database management systems (DBMSs). It is now clear the SQL is the winner. IBM has declared SQL its database language for the Systems Application Architecture (SAA). The strong industry support for SQL has resulted in its emergence as the undisputed language for medium- and large-scale DBMSs. SQL has made significant inroads in the microcomputer world: popular packages such as dBASE and RBase now support SQL. As a result, the gap between end users and data-processing professionals will be narrowed, as they will now speak the same language.

This text is an introduction to Standard SQL as defined by American National Standards Institute (ANSI). In addition, it extends to include the language as it is incorporated in DB2 and ORACLE. This book covers the various aspects of creating and manipulating a database, presenting them simply to arouse the interest of the database user.

The first chapter introduces relational database systems concepts; subsequent chapters discuss the SQL language. Chapter 2 describes the creation of a database using SQL. Chapters 3 and 4 illustrate the components of the SQL **SELECT** statement step-by-step, using more than fifty examples. Data retrieval and update instructions are addressed here. Later chapters cover more advanced features: referential integrity, views, indexes, security, transaction control, and the system catalog. Chapter 8 introduces the reader to Embedded SQL and its cursor concept for managing data access within the constraints of typical programming languages. Chapters 1 through 8 have exercises; answers to selected odd-numbered questions appear at the end of the text.

Part B presents three relational database systems: DB2, OR-ACLE, and dBASE. These systems are used here because students are likely to encounter them at work or at school. The objective of Part B is to expose students to popular commercial SQL products in different environments. By reviewing the material in Part B and practicing the various examples, students will gain an understanding of SQL. The chapters on ORACLE and dBASE IV lend themselves very well to a self-paced, hands-on, live SQL experience.

Two case studies are used throughout the text: the library database illustrates SQL, the banking database augments the exercises. Since library and banking examples are familiar to all readers and affect them in their day-to-day lives, they should give the students a practical, working knowledge of SQL.

Appendix A presents the banking database. Appendix B consists of SQL Command Language statements, and is a valuable reference source.

Both authors have worked with and have taught database systems for several years. Both authors felt the need for a text that covers SQL in greater depth than is typically found in available textbooks. Consequently, this book is useful to students enrolled in Computer Science, Information Systems, and Business Computing courses, in addition to Database Systems courses. In a full course, Part A and at least one of the three commercial systems discussed in Part B should be studied. In an introductory course, chapter 8 and Part B may be omitted (unless you are using dBASE, ORACLE, or DB2). This book can also be used as a stand-alone text in a two-to four-day SQL seminar.

This book will also be of value to the database systems professional or the end user who wants a better understanding of SQL. Systems analysts and programmers involved in design and implementation of database applications will also find the presentation on Embedded SQL very useful. This is covered in chapter 8, which provides both COBOL and PL/I examples; and in chapter 10, which uses dBASE IV SQL.

A diskette containing SQL CREATE / INSERT commands, based on the library database, formatted for dBASE IV and ORACLE is available upon request from our publisher, Wm. C. Brown.

Acknowledgements

We are grateful to our students who used preliminary versions of this text, and provided useful suggestions. We would like to acknowledge Bina Thakkar for her contribution in chapter 10. We would like to thank many people at Wm. C. Brown who were directly involved in the production of this book, especially Matt Loeb, Darlene Schueller and Carla Arnold. We would like to thank various referees for their constructive criticism of the early draft of the manuscript, and the following individuals who reviewed the book: William R. Cornette, Southwest Missouri State University; William H. Crouch, Old Dominion University; and Pentti A. Honkanen, Georgia State University. Finally, we would like to thank our various colleagues at the University of Manitoba and University of Winnipeg for their encouragement and support.

Part

Structured Query Language (SQL)

1

Introduction

This chapter presents an overview of a relational database system. Relations (tables) and the use of SQL for accessing data in a relational database are introduced.

1.1 Introduction

Most organizations today store their data resource in a database. A *database* is a central reservoir for all data.

A computerized database facilitates sharing of data and information. Consider a *library users* database. Any branch of the same library should be capable of checking your book in or out. Each branch should also be able to answer questions such as How much do I owe in fines? or Is this book available? In order to respond to such questions, the library database should be available at all the branches.

Databases have to be queried and updated frequently—new data inserted, old data removed, and existing data changed. A Data Base Management System (DBMS) is used to facilitate these tasks. It enables storage, retrieval, and manipulation of the database.

1.2 The Relational Model

The relational model is the almost exclusive choice for implementation and use on a microcomputer. The model is simple, flexible, and easy to use. Consider a database as a collection of tables. Each table is a two-dimensional construct of rows and columns. The mathematical concept comparable to the term *table* is *relation*. Hence, the name *relational database*.

Consider the sample table shown below. The first book has call number *100* , title *Physics Handbook* and subject category *Physics*. The information for each book is stored in rows, which are sometimes called *records* or, more formally, *tuples*. The columns define *fields*: TITLE field, SUBJECT field, etc. A field is also called an *attribute*.

Call_no	Title	Subject
100	Physics Handbook	Physics
200	Database Systems	Computing
300	Modula-2	Computing
400	Database Design	Computing
500	Software Testing	Computing
600	Business Society	Business
700	Graphs	Mathematics
800	Cell Biology	Biology
900	Set Theory	Mathematics

In the relational model, each row should have a unique identifier—a *primary key*. For example, each *call number* is a unique identifier in the table above. When a specific value is given as the primary key, it identifies a single row. Generally speaking, one does not put information into a database unless it is possible to recall it later. In this manner, each book and each library patron is uniquely identified.

A language is needed to define and access information in the database and to retrieve and update the data. In this book we discuss Structured Query Language (SQL) for accessing data in a relational database.

1.3 Structured Query Language (SQL)

Every DBMS has a data sublanguage embedded in its architecture that it uses to communicate with the database. The data-sublanguage commands can be classified by type of operation performed:

a Data Definition Language (DDL) that facilitates the creation and description of a database; a Data Manipulation Language (DML) that deals with the manipulation of the data; and a Data Control Language (DCL) that specifies security constraints.

The SQL language is comprised of:

1. **DDL:** data definition language. DDL is used to define the tables that make up the database. Chapters 2, 5, 6, and the section on indexes in chapter 7 discuss aspects of the DDL.

2. **DML:** data manipulation language. DML is concerned with the retrieval and update of the database. Chapters 3 and 4 discuss the DML. Chapter 8 discusses the use of SQL within standard programming languages such as COBOL and PL/I.

3. **DCL:** data control language. DCL is used to specify who can access data in the database and what operations they can perform. The section on DCL in chapter 7 discusses controlling access in SQL databases.

SQL, often pronounced *sequel*, is based on a data language initially designed for the IBM prototype relational database system called System R. SQL has been standardized by ANSI and will continue to be enhanced; when appropriate we make references to the standard ANSI SQL. It has been adopted as an industry standard for relational database systems. Such systems appear on microcomputers, minicomputers, and mainframes; in some cases the same product is available on all three. The number of SQL database systems is enormous and growing; the list includes IBM's SQL/DS and DB2, Relational Technologies' INGRES, Oracle Corporation's ORACLE, Cincom's SUPRA, and Ashton-Tate's dBASE IV.

1.4 Summary

We have introduced the relational model. A *relational database* consists of *tables*, very simple data structures that everyone can understand. Every database system requires a language for accessing data; the language discussed in this text is SQL and its sublanguages

DDL, DML, and DCL. Every table should have a *primary key* to access database information.

Exercises

1.1 What is a database? What is a DBMS?

1.2 Describe the early history of relational database management systems.

1.3 What does SQL stand for? Who introduced it and when?

1.4 What are the advantages of having a standard query language?

1.5 Research into advantages and disadvantages of SQL.

1.6 Briefly describe any five popular relational DBMS systems.

1.7 Name two popular DBMS systems and their vendors in each of the following categories: a) Hierarchical, b) Network, and c) Relational.

1.8 What are the advantages of relational database systems over hierarchical and network?

2
Defining the Database

The database is a collection of tables. Each table is a two dimensional structure of rows and columns. A row is sometimes called a *record* and a column is sometimes called a *field* (these terms are carried over from data processing). The DDL is used to define (create) tables, views, and indexes.

Tables are created in accordance with data management needs, and as these needs grow, it may be necessary to add new fields to existing tables.

A *view* is a virtual table defined in terms of other tables—it does not occupy any real space in the database. The view mechanism is very powerful and useful; it can simplify a user's perception of the database, and it can provide some types of security.

Indexes provide the database system with efficient access paths to rows of tables. They are created to improve the efficiency of data requests.

This chapter concentrates on the **CREATE TABLE** command; later chapters discuss views and indexes.

2.1 The Library Database

A sample database consisting of three tables used in a library will illustrate features of SQL:

BOOK

Information on each book in the library is recorded in the BOOK table:

BOOK: call_no   title   subject

For each book there is

- a call number (*call_no*) which uniquely identifies the book
- the *title* of the book
- the *subject* matter of the book

LOAN

Each time a book is borrowed, information is recorded in the LOAN table:

LOAN: call_no   user_id   date_due   date_ret   fine   paid

For each loan of a book to a person, the following are recorded:

- the call number (*call_no*) of the book borrowed
- the identifier (*user_id*) of the person borrowing the book
- the date the book is due (*due_date*)
- the date the book was returned (*date_ret*); no value is assigned until the book is returned
- the *fine* for all books returned late, calculated at the rate of 10 cents per day (no value is assigned until the book is actually returned)
- the attribute *paid*; if its value is *yes*, the fine has been paid

The LOAN table is illustrated in Figure 2.1. Note the following:

- Three cases in which a book has not been returned:

○ *user-id* 100 has not returned the book with *call_no* 300

○ *user_id* 250 has not returned the book with *call_no* 500

○ *user_id* 400 has not returned the book with *call_no* 900

• Two cases in which a book was returned before the due date:

○ *user_id* 100 returned *call_no* 100

○ *user_id* 300 returned *call_no* 700

• Five cases in which a book was returned late:

○ fines were assessed and paid.

PATRON

For each library user, or patron, information is recorded in the PATRON table:

PATRON: **user_id**   **name**   **age**

Each patron has

• an identification number (ID) which uniquely identifies him (*user_id*)

• his *name*

• his *age*

This database represents a subset of the information requirements of any library. The contents of the library database are illustrated in Figure 2.1.

Figure 2.1   Contents of tables in the database.

BOOK

call_no	title	subject
100	Physics Handbook	Physics
200	Database Systems	Computing
300	Modula-2	Computing
400	Database Design	Computing
500	Software Testing	Computing
600	Business Society	Business
700	Graphs	Mathematics
800	Cell Biology	Biology
900	Set Theory	Mathematics

LOAN

call_no	user_id	date_due	date_ret	fine	paid
100	100	12-SEP-88	01-SEP-88		
300	100	01-SEP-88			
900	200	01-SEP-88	20-DEC-88	1.90	yes
400	200	04-DEC-89	16-MAY-90	16.30	yes
600	200	04-DEC-89	16-MAY-90	16.30	yes
500	250	02-OCT-84			
600	250	02-OCT-84	02-OCT-85	36.50	yes
700	300	10-DEC-88	01-DEC-88		
800	350	01-DEC-88	30-DEC-88	2.90	yes
900	400	01-OCT-90			

PATRON

user_id	name	age
100	Wong	22
150	Colin	31
200	King	21
250	Das	67
300	Niall	17
350	Smith	72
400	Jones	41

2.2 Creating Tables

To create a table one uses the **CREATE TABLE** command. The syntax is

> **CREATE TABLE** table-name
>   (column-specifications);

The table is named (*table-name*) and each column is defined (*column-specification*). A *column-specification* defines the column by giving its data type and its other properties. The execution of this command causes the system to save the definition of the table, which is initially empty. We shall now illustrate the use of the command and then we shall discuss data types and other options. To create the BOOK table:

> **CREATE TABLE** BOOK (
>   call_no   **INTEGER,**
>   title   **CHARACTER** (30),
>   subject   **CHARACTER** (12));

Three columns have now been defined for the BOOK table: *call_no, title,* and *subject. Call_no* is defined as a number (integer); *title* and *subject* are defined as character strings of lengths 30 and 12 respectively. The specification of data type is required and is restrictive. Once *call_no* has been defined as an integer, a call number of QA76.9 is impossible, since it is not a number. Book titles and subjects must be enclosed in single quotes: 'Introduction to Database Systems'.

2.2.1 Data types

ANSI SQL has eight data types: **CHARACTER, NUMERIC, DECIMAL, INTEGER, SMALL INTEGER, FLOAT, REAL**, and **DOUBLE PRECISION**. A SQL system may not provide all these types, and may include others. Most systems provide additional types that really are necessary (SQL might be considered deficient on this) such as **MONEY, DATE** and **TIME.**
    Some SQL systems simplify the choices; ORACLE, for instance, places all the numeric types into one category: **NUMBER**. When

using a SQL system, it is best to refer to its documentation to determine the data types available.

2.2.2 **NOT NULL** and **UNIQUE**

ANSI SQL specifies two additional properties that can be specified for a column: **NOT NULL**, and **UNIQUE**. If **NOT NULL** is specified for a column, whenever a row is inserted or updated, that column must have a value assigned to it. **Null** is a special term used when a field has never been assigned a value and its value is unknown or missing. **Null** is not the same as blank characters or zero value. If we specify **UNIQUE** for a column, then every row in the table must have a unique value in that column. (DB2 does not allow the **UNIQUE** property to be specified in the table definition; but one can achieve this by creating a unique index [see the chapter on indexing]. We shall not use **UNIQUE** in our examples.)

Let's consider the BOOK table again. Standard library practice demands that a book have a call number to be placed in the library. Each book has a title and a subject assigned in the cataloging process. A suitable definition of the BOOK table would be

```
CREATE TABLE BOOK (
    call_no      INTEGER           NOT NULL,
    title        CHARACTER (30)    NOT NULL,
    subject      CHARACTER(12)     NOT NULL);
```

Suitable definitions for the PATRON table and the LOAN tables would be

```
CREATE TABLE PATRON (
    user_id      INTEGER           NOT NULL,
    name         CHARACTER(30)     NOT NULL,
    age          INTEGER );

CREATE TABLE LOAN (
    call_no      INTEGER           NOT NULL,
    user_id      INTEGER           NOT NULL,
    date_due     DATE              NOT NULL,
    date_ret     DATE,
    fine         MONEY,
    paid         CHARACTER(3));
```

In this example, the *DATE* and *MONEY* data types available in many systems are used. If they are not available in your particular system, use one of the numeric types instead.

2.3 Altering Tables

Most SQL systems have a command to incorporate new columns in an existing table. For instance, to add a new column for addresses to the PATRON table, one would use the following command:

ALTER TABLE PATRON
ADD address *CHARACTER* (30);

The **ALTER TABLE** command can be used for other purposes, such as changing the column length or adding a property such as **NOT NULL;** however, this may only be allowed in very restricted cases.

2.4 Dropping Tables

To remove or drop a table from the database, the DROP TABLE command is used. To remove the BOOK table, one executes the command:

DROP TABLE BOOK;

This command is very powerful: all rows in the table are deleted and the table disappears.

2.5 Copying Tables

Some SQL systems, such as ORACLE, allow the creation of a new table from an old one using *CREATE TABLE* with a *subquery*. Queries or **SELECT** statements, are discussed in greater detail in chapter 3. To create a new table SENIORS of patrons, age 65 or older, from the PATRON table:

```
CREATE TABLE SENIORS
AS
        SELECT FROM PATRON
        WHERE age > = 65;
```

and a table would be created with the following rows:

user_id	name	age
250	Das	67
350	Smith	72

The table inherited the column titles of the PATRON table since no other titles were named. In some cases, the column would need to be named. For instance, a table giving the call number, user ID, and the number of days the book was kept could be derived from the LOAN table:

```
CREATE TABLE DAYSKEPT (call_no, user_id, kept)
AS
        SELECT (call_no, user_id, date_ret - date_due)
        FROM LOAN;
```

Exercises

The questions in this exercise are based on the International Bank case study described in Appendix A.

2.1 Using SQL, create the following tables (use **NOT NULL**where appropriate):

a) CUSTOMER table

b) ACCOUNT table

c) TRANSACTION table

2.2 Display the structure of the tables that you have just created.

2.3 Add the sample records described in Appendix A to the CUSTOMER table, ACCOUNT table, and the TRANSACTION table. (Chapter 9 describes how this is done using ORACLE, chapter 10 using dBASE, and chapter 4 using any other database system.)

2.4 Write SQL statements that will modify the CUSTOMER table to include a new column called **phone**. Assume it to be a character field of size 14.

2.5 What SQL syntax will delete the TRANSACTION table?

2.6 Will your DBMS let you delete columns or modify the data type (and size) when

a) no data has yet been added to the table?

b) data has already been added?

3

Data Manipulation: SQL Queries

The **SELECT** command is primarily used to retrieve data from the database. It is also used to create copies of tables, to create views, and to specify rows for updating. This chapter concentrates on its use for retrieving data.

The basic form of the **SELECT** is

> **SELECT** field-list
> **FROM** table-list
> **WHERE** field-expression
> **GROUP BY** group-fields
> **HAVING** group-expression
> **ORDER BY** field-list;

The result of the **SELECT** is a listing of data derived from some set of tables in the database. The *field list* specifies the fields to be listed, such as *user_id, name, age*. The data listed is obtained from the set of tables (*table-list*) specified in the **FROM** clause. The *field-expression* in the **WHERE** clause specifies a logical expression that rows in the *table-list* must satisfy to be included in the listing. The **GROUP BY** clause is used when we wish to summarize information in the underlying tables. For example, "**GROUP BY subject**" causes the rows to be organized into groups, one group for each unique value of the subject field. The **HAVING** clause is used to specify which groups are to be included. **ORDER BY** is used to sequence the rows of the listing. The **WHERE, GROUP BY, HAVING**, and **ORDER BY** clauses are optional.

3.1 Simple Queries

We illustrate queries that retrieve all rows of a table.

Example 3.1   List the titles of books in the database.

>   **SELECT** title
>   **FROM** BOOK;

   When an SQL system executes the above example, it accesses the BOOK table. Since the **SELECT** does not involve a **WHERE** clause, all rows of BOOK are accessed. The system extracts and displays the title from all rows; there are as many rows in the result as there are rows in BOOK:

>   **Result:**   title
>
>   Physics Handbook
>   Database Systems
>   Modula-2
>   Database Design
>   Software Testing
>   Business Society
>   Graphs
>   Cell Biology
>   Set Theory

Example 3.2   List the title and subject for each book.

>   **SELECT** title, subject
>   **FROM** BOOK;

>   **Result:**   title   subject
>
>   Physics Handbook   Physics
>   Database Systems   Computing
>   Modula-2   Computing
>   Database Design   Computing
>   Software Testing   Computing
>   Business Society   Business
>   Graphs   Mathematics
>   Cell Biology   Biology
>   Set Theory   Mathematics

Example 3.3 List all fields for each book.

a) **SELECT** call_no, title, subject

   FROM BOOK;

b) **SELECT** *

   FROM BOOK;

   (* is a symbol for *all fields*.)

Result:	Call_no	title	subject
	100	Physics Handbook	Physics
	200	Database Systems	Computing
	300	Modula-2	Computing
	400	Database Design	Computing
	500	Software Testing	Computing
	600	Business Society	Business
	700	Graphs	Mathematics
	800	Cell Biology	Biology
	900	Set Theory	Mathematics

Example 3.4 What are the subject areas of the library?

    SELECT subject
    FROM BOOK;

Result:	subject
	Physics
	Computing
	Computing
	Computing
	Computing
	Business
	Mathematics
	Biology
	Mathematics

The answer to this query has as many lines as there are books in the library. Since there are only a few subject areas, the result looks awkward. To remove the redundancies from the display, use the **DISTINCT** function, which eliminates redundant rows.

> **SELECT DISTINCT** subject
> **FROM** BOOK;

> Result: subject
>
> > Biology
> > Business
> > Computing
> > Mathematics
> > Physics

3.2 Selecting Rows

In the previous section we were concerned with listing one or more fields from a table; every row of the table corresponded to a line in the listing. Now we consider the retrieval of a subset of the rows of a table. To limit the retrieval to specific rows, we include the **WHERE** clause in our commands. The **WHERE** clause gives the condition that a row must satisfy to be included; any row of the table not satisfying the condition is not retrieved. Operators that may appear in conditions are

> =,   < >,   >,   > =,   <,   < =
> **IN**
> **BETWEEN** . . .   **AND** . . .
> **LIKE**
> **IS NULL**
> **AND, OR, NOT**

Example 3.5 List the titles of Mathematics books.

> **SELECT** title
> **FROM** BOOK
> **WHERE** subject = 'Mathematics';

Result: **title**

                    Graphs
                    Set Theory

The condition "*subject* = 'Mathematics' " is evaluated for each row of BOOK. If the expression evaluates to *True* then the row is listed in the result.

Example 3.6   List the book with call number 200.

        SELECT title
        FROM BOOK
        WHERE call_no = 200;

Result: **title**

                    Database Systems

3.3 Arithmetic Operators

The standard operators +, −,   *, and /   are available for addition, subtraction, multiplication, and division respectively. These can be applied to fields being retrieved or to fields within the WHERE clause. Use parentheses to force or clarify the order of computation, because expressions in parentheses are evaluated first. An expression is evaluated from left to right unless parentheses or priorities dictate otherwise. * and / have equal priority; likewise + and − have equal priority. However, * and / have higher priority than + and −; hence they are computed first.

Example 3.7   List patrons fines in British pounds (assuming one pound is equivalent to two dollars).

        SELECT call_no, user_id, fine*0.5
        FROM LOAN;

Result:	call_no	user_id	fine*0.5
	100	100	
	300	100	
	900	200	0.95
	400	200	8.15
	600	200	8.15
	500	250	
	600	250	18.25
	700	300	
	800	350	1.45
	900	400	

Example 3.8   List loans where the fine is over 10 British pounds.

```
SELECT *
FROM LOAN
WHERE (fine*0.5) > 10.00;
```

Result:

call_no	user_id	date_due	date_ret	fine	paid
600	250	02-OCT-84	02-OCT-85	36.50	yes

3.4 Boolean Operators

The condition specified in the **WHERE** clause can be a Boolean expression that involves **AND, OR** and **NOT**. The priority of the Boolean operators from highest to lowest is **NOT, AND, OR.** Of course, parentheses can be used to clarify or force evaluation to be performed in a certain order.

Example 3.9   List the call numbers of books borrowed by patron 200 or patron 250 and where the fine paid is greater than $2.00.

```
SELECT DISTINCT call_no
FROM LOAN
WHERE fine > 2.00
AND (user_id =  200 OR user_id = 250);
```

Result:　　　　call_no

400

600

3.5 Special Operators for the WHERE Clause

Four operators are available to handle special cases:

LIKE is used when searching for a particular character string.

BETWEEN is used when searching for a value within some range.

IS NULL is used to test for a field's not having been assigned any value.

IN is used to test for a field's having a value contained in some set of values.

3.5.1 LIKE

LIKE is used with character data to determine the presence of a substring. Special notations are available to specify unknown or irrelevant characters in the field being tested:

a single unknown character: _ (underscore)
any number of unknown characters: %

Example 3.10 List books with *Database* in the title.

```
SELECT *
FROM BOOK
WHERE title LIKE ' % Database % ';
```

Result:	call_no	title	subject
	200	Database Systems	Computing
	400	Database Design	Computing

Each BOOK title is examined to determine if it contains the character string *Database*.

Example 3.11   List books with titles having an **o** as the second character.

> **SELECT** *
> **FROM** BOOK
> **WHERE** title **LIKE** ' _ o % ' ;

> Result: call_no   title   subject
>
> 300   Modula-2   Computing
> 500   Software Testing   Computing

The title field of each row in BOOK is examined to determine if it has an *o* in the second character position.

3.5.2 BETWEEN

The **BETWEEN** operator is used with numeric data to determine if the data in a field lies within a certain range.

Example 3.12   List books with call numbers between 200 and 400.

> **SELECT** *
> **FROM** BOOK
> **WHERE** call_no **BETWEEN** 200 **AND** 400;

> Result: call_no   title   subject
>
> 200   Database Systems   Computing
> 300   Modula-2   Computing
> 400   Database Design   Computing

Note that this is the same as the command:

> **SELECT** *
> **FROM** BOOK
> **WHERE** (call_no > = 200) **AND** (call_no < = 400);

3.5.3 IS NULL

NULL is the keyword used to determine whether or not a field has been assigned a value. Note that in our database the *date returned* field is not assigned any value until a book is returned. If a book is returned on time, then no value is assigned to the *fine* or *paid* fields.

Example 3.13 List the books currently out on loan.

> **SELECT** call_no
> **FROM** LOAN
> **WHERE** date_ret **IS NULL**;

> Result: call_no
>   300
>   500
>   900

Example 3.14 List the books that have been returned by patron 100.

> **SELECT** call_no
> **FROM** LOAN
> **WHERE** (user_id = 100) **AND** (date_ret **IS NOT NULL**);

> Result: call_no
>   100

IS NOT NULL is the expression used to determine if a field of a row has been assigned a value. It is not permitted to use the expression "*date_ret = NULL*" and "*date_ret < > NULL*".

3.5.4 IN

The set of values used for comparison can be explicitly specified as illustrated here. (They can be given as a *subquery* also; subqueries will be discussed later.)

Example 3.15   List the names of patrons whose *user_id* is *100,
200, 300,* or *350.*

> **SELECT** name
> **FROM** PATRON
> **WHERE** user_id **IN** (100,200,300,350);

> **Result:**   **name**
>
>   Wong
>   King
>   Niall
>   Smith

The list of values used for comparison are enclosed in parentheses. The patron's name is listed if the *user_id* is in the list.

Example 3.16   List all **Computing** and **History** titles.

> **SELECT** title
> **FROM** BOOK
> **WHERE** subject **IN** ('Computing', 'History');

> **Result:**   **title**
>
>   Database Systems
>   Modula-2
>   Database Design
>   Software Testing

Note that our database does not happen to contain any books
in the *History* category.

3.6 System Variables

SQL systems have system variables that are used to hold values
of general use or interest. All systems have the variable **USER** which
holds the current logged-on user's ID. The **USER** variable can be
incorporated into the database by relating it to a column of one
or more of the tables. **USER** determines if the person logged-on

has the necessary access privileges to carry out his requests (See the section on DCL).

Systems like DB2 have many other variables such as **CURRENT DATE, CURRENT TIME, CURRENT TIMESTAMP, CURRENT TIMEZONE.** ORACLE has a variable **SYSDATE** which can be used to determine the current time and date.

Example 3.17   List patrons who have outstanding books.

We shall use DB2's **CURRENT DATE** in this example. Any system which includes date as a data type would likely permit arithmetic operations and comparisons (DB2 does).

```
SELECT user_id
FROM LOAN
WHERE date_ret IS NULL
AND CURRENT DATE > date_due;
```

Result: user_id

                 100
                 250

3.7   Column Functions (Aggregate Functions)*

SQL offers special functions, all called *aggregate* functions, to determine maximums, minimums, averages, totals and counts for entire columns. These are **MAX, MIN, AVG, SUM** and **COUNT** respectively. Note that **AVG** and **SUM** are defined for numeric values only, and that their computations exclude NULL values.

Example 3.18   What is the largest fine paid for an overdue book?

```
SELECT MAX (fine)
FROM LOAN;
```

Result: max (fine)

                 36.50

Example 3.19   How much has the library assessed in fines?

> **SELECT SUM**(fine)
> **FROM** LOAN;

    Result: sum(fine)

                                 73.90

3.7.1 Use of COUNT

ANSI SQL specifies that **COUNT** can be used in only two ways. First, we can use **COUNT(*)** to count the number of rows which satisfy a query. Second, we can use **COUNT** with **DISTINCT** to count the number of unique values in a column (see section 3.7.2).

Example 3.20   How many books are in the library?

> **SELECT COUNT(*)**
> **FROM** BOOK;

    Result: count(*)

                                 9

This use of **COUNT** for counting rows does not involve any elimination of NULL values. That is, if a row has all NULL values it will be counted.

Example 3.21   How many times has a fine been assessed?

> **SELECT COUNT(*)**
> **FROM** LOAN
> **WHERE** fine **IS NOT NULL**;

    Result: count(fine)

                                 5

Example 3.22 How many **Computing** books are there?

> SELECT COUNT(*)
> FROM BOOK
> WHERE subject = 'Computing';

Result: count(call_no)

                       4

3.7.2 Use of DISTINCT

ANSI SQL permits the specifications of **DISTINCT** with an aggregate function; the effect is to remove duplicate values before the function is applied.

Example 3.23 How many subject areas are there?

> SELECT COUNT(DISTINCT subject)
> FROM BOOK;

Result: count(distinct subject)

           5

Example 3.24 How many patrons have borrowed books?

> SELECT COUNT(DISTINCT user_id)
> FROM LOAN;

Result: count(distinct user_id)

                       6

Whenever **DISTINCT** is used, the argument must be a simple field reference as shown above.

3.8 Ordering the Result

The **ORDER BY** clause is used to force the result to be ordered by one or more column values in either ascending or descending order.

Example 3.25   List books in alphabetical order by title.

```
SELECT call_no, title, subject
FROM BOOK
ORDER BY title;
```

Result:	call_no	title	subject
	600	Business Society	Business
	800	Cell Biology	Biology
	400	Database Design	Computing
	200	Database Systems	Computing
	700	Graphs	Mathematics
	300	Modula-2	Computing
	100	Physics Handbook	Physics
	900	Set Theory	Mathematics
	500	Software Testing	Computing

The default is ascending order; this could be specified explicitly by coding **"ORDER BY title ASC"**. Instead of specifying a field name, we can refer to it indirectly by its relative position in the field-list. For the above we could have used: **"ORDER BY 2"**.

Example 3.26   List books in subject order, and, with each subject, order them by call number.

```
SELECT *
FROM BOOK
ORDER BY subject ASC, call_no DESC;
```

Result:	call_no	title	subject
	800	Cell Biology	Biology
	600	Business Society	Business
	500	Software Testing	Computing
	400	Database Design	Computing
	300	Modula-2	Computing
	200	Database Systems	Computing
	900	Set Theory	Mathematics
	700	Graphs	Mathematics
	100	Physics Handbook	Physics

Note that the result is ordered first by subject: *Biology* is first, followed by *Business*, then *Computing*, and finally *Mathematics*. Within each group, the ordering is by call number.

3.9 Grouping Data

The **GROUP BY** clause is used to specify one or more fields that are to be used for organizing rows into groups. Rows that have the same value(s) are grouped together for the specified field(s). The only simple fields that can be displayed are the ones used for grouping; any result from other fields must be specified using a column function. The column function will be applied to a group of rows instead of to the entire table.

Example 3.27   For each patron, list the number of books he has borrowed.

```
SELECT uscr_id, COUNT(*)
FROM LOAN
GROUP BY user_id;
```

Result:	user_id	count(*)
	100	2
	200	3
	250	2
	300	1
	350	1
	400	1

The effect of this **SELECT** is to

1. cause the SQL system to group the rows of loan by *user_id*
2. display the *user_id* for each group and a count of the rows in the group

A common error is to include a field in the listing that is not unique for the group. For example,

> **SELECT** user_id, call_no, **COUNT(*)**
> **FROM** LOAN
> **GROUP BY** user_id;

would be incorrect because *call_no* is not single-valued for a group. When **GROUP BY** is used, each element of the **SELECT** list must be single-valued; each element must either be specified in the **GROUP BY** statement or be the result of a column function.

Example 3.28 For each patron, list total fines paid.

> **SELECT** user_id, **SUM**(fine)
> **FROM** LOAN
> **GROUP BY** user_id;

Result:	user_id	sum(fine)
	100	
	200	34.50
	250	36.50
	300	
	350	2.90
	400	

We see that some patrons who have not paid a fine are listed anyway. To exclude rows from the grouping process (and from the **SELECT**), the appropriate **WHERE** clause must be specified.

Example 3.29 For each patron who has paid a fine, list his total.

```
SELECT user_id, SUM(fine)
FROM LOAN
WHERE fine IS NOT NULL
GROUP BY user_id;
```

Result:	user_id	sum(fine)
	200	34.50
	250	36.50
	350	2.90

The only difference between Example 3.28 and 3.29 is that Example 3.29 does not report patrons who have not paid any fines.

3.9.1 Restricting groups using HAVING

In the foregoing examples, all groups have been reported. To eliminate groups from the result, we use the **HAVING** clause to specify an appropriate group-oriented Boolean expression.

Example 3.30   List the patron IDs for those who have paid more than $30 in fines on books with call numbers greater than 400.

```
SELECT user_id
FROM LOAN
WHERE call_no > 400
GROUP BY user_id
HAVING SUM (fine) > 30;
```

Result:	user_id
	250

3.9.2 Interaction of clauses in the SELECT

The previous example has used all components of the **SELECT** command. It is important to understand the priority, or the order in which the **SELECT** statement is processed.

- The **WHERE** is done first
- **GROUP BY** second, and
- **HAVING** third.

The rows of LOAN are accessed; each row of LOAN which satisfies the **WHERE** clause is retained for further processing (the grouping). Only those rows of LOAN which correspond to books with call numbers larger than 400 are retained. These rows are organized into groups according to the specifications in the **GROUP BY** clause. In this case, the rows are grouped by *user_id*. When a **HAVING** clause is present, each group must satisfy the condition in order to be displayed in the result. In this case, each group must have a fine total greater than $30.

3.10 Joins

A join is performed when a **SELECT** statement specifies more than one table in the **FROM** clause. It is used when it is necessary to retrieve information from more than one table.

Example 3.31   List the names of patrons, their IDs, and the call numbers of the books they have borrowed.

Two tables must be used to get the information: PATRON and LOAN. A row of PATRON should be matched with a row of LOAN whenever they have the same value in the *user_id* field. Since a patron is expected to borrow many books, one row of PATRON can be matched with many rows of LOAN. With SQL, it is necessary to specify this join condition explicitly:

```
SELECT patron.name, patron.user_id, loan.call_no
FROM PATRON, LOAN
WHERE patron.user_id = loan.user_id;
```

Result:	patron.name	patron.user_id	loan.call_no
	Wong	100	100
	Wong	100	300
	King	200	900
	King	200	400
	King	200	600
	Das	250	500
	Das	250	600
	Niall	300	700
	Smith	350	800
	Jones	400	900

Note that we have used prefixes for our field specifications. This is only necessary whenever there would be ambiguity regarding the table where the field appears. In this case prefixes are only necessary for the *user_id* field.

If we forgot to include the clause

> **WHERE** patron.user_id = loan.user_id

and had just typed

> **SELECT** patron.name, patron.user_id, loan.call_no
> **FROM** PATRON, LOAN

our **SELECT** would have produced a result called a *cartesian product*. For our sample database, there would have been 7 x 10 = 70 rows in the result, since PATRON has 7 rows and LOAN has 10 rows. Without the **WHERE** clause, each row of **PATRON** would be joined with every row of **LOAN**.

Example 3.32 List the names of patrons who have books out on loan.

The information needed to do this is found in two tables: LOAN contains the record of books loaned out (specifically we are interested in those rows where the *date_ret* column has no value), and PATRON contains the name for each patron. We need to match up a selected row of LOAN with the pertinent row of PATRON. This is done by requiring them to have the same value for the *user_id* field.

> **SELECT** name
> **FROM** LOAN, PATRON
> **WHERE** loan.date_ret **IS NULL**
> **AND** loan.user_id = patron.user_id;

Result: **name**

> Wong
> Das
> Jones

3.10.1 Aliases

It is sometimes necessary and often convenient to use an alias (an alternative name) for a table. An alias is specified in the **FROM** clause immediately following the actual table name. In the next example, we need the alias because a table is joined with itself—called a *self-join*. It may be useful to think of the join as being performed on two copies of the same table.

Example 3.33   List each patron's name and the number of other patrons older than he/she.

In the following, one "copy" of the PATRON table is referred to as **a**; the other as **b**.

> **SELECT** a.name, **COUNT(*)**
> **FROM** PATRON a, PATRON b
> **WHERE** a.age < b.age
> **GROUP BY** a.user_id, a.name;

Result: **a.name**   **count(*)**

a.name	count(*)
Wong	4
Colin	3
King	5
Das	1
Niall	6
Jones	2

Note the **GROUP BY** clause in the example; it illustrates an important point regarding the *elements* listed by the query. We have grouped the response using two fields; *user_id* and *name*. In the **SELECT** clause we have included *name* and **COUNT(*)**. If we grouped only by *user_id*, then *name* would not be considered by SQL to be single-valued for each group. As far as SQL is concerned, *name* could have a different value in each row of a group. Everything included in the **SELECT** must be single-valued for a group when **GROUP BY** is used. Note in the result for example 3.33 that Smith does not appear. The row for Smith was not joined with any row.

3.10.2 Outer Join

ANSI SQL does not provide for the outer join operation, a useful form of join for many situations. Some systems (such as ORACLE) provide the outer join, and other systems (such as DB2) do not. Let us examine the very simple database request:

For each book in the library, list its title and the number of times it has been loaned out.

One approach (an incorrect one) that comes quickly to mind is

```
SELECT title, COUNT(*)
FROM BOOK b, LOAN l
WHERE b.call_no = l.call_no
GROUP BY b.call_no, title;
```

This query does give us correct counts for those books that have been loaned out, but nothing is listed for books that have never been loaned out at all. Such books will not be matched to any row of LOAN and, therefore, do not contribute to the result.

Let us consider now how ORACLE and the outer join can be used to formulate a simple and correct query. In the **WHERE** clause, in which the join condition is specified (b.call_no = l.call_no), ORACLE allows us to place a (+) to designate a column which is to be matched with an imaginary row of NULLs if there are no other matches. Instead of specifying "**COUNT(*)**" we specify "**COUNT**(l.user_id)":

```
SELECT title, COUNT(l.user_id)
FROM BOOK b, LOAN l
WHERE b.call_no = l.call_no(+)
GROUP BY b.call_no, title;
```

If a row of BOOK is not matched on call number to a row of LOAN, it will be matched to an imaginary row where all column values are NULL. Hence, every row of BOOK is matched to something, and the title and a count will be produced. Note that ORACLE permits "COUNT(l.user_id)" to be specified without DISTINCT. ORACLE's COUNT(. . .) ignores NULL's and produces a value of zero when a book is matched to a row of NULLs.

In those systems where the outer join is not available, the same result can be obtained by using the following query (that contains a complicated subquery using EXISTS (see section 3.11).

```
SELECT title, COUNT(*)
FROM BOOK b, LOAN l
WHERE b.call_no = l.call_no
GROUP BY b.call_no, title;

UNION

SELECT title, 0
FROM BOOK b
WHERE NOT EXISTS
      (SELECT * FROM LOAN l
      WHERE l.call_no = b.call_no);
```

When UNION is used to obtain the result, it would probably be more efficient to use UNION ALL since there are no duplicate rows to be eliminated. (See section 3.12 for more information on UNION.)

3.11 Nested Queries

SQL allows the nesting of one query inside another, but only in the WHERE clause and the HAVING clause. ANSI SQL permits a

subquery only on the right hand side of an operator. The operators available are **IN, EXISTS**, and the relational operators: =, <
>, >, > =, <, < =. SQL allows the use of a relational operator when
a subquery will return just a single row (normally a single field
value). When a subquery returns more than one row (a set of rows),
a relational operator *must* be used with *ALL* or *ANY*.

3.11.1 Use of IN

The **IN** operator is used to determine if some value is present in
a list of values. That list can be explicitly specified (covered previously) or generated by a subquery.

Example 3.34   List names and ages of patrons who have books
out on loan.

We shall give two separate queries to accomplish this and then
specify it as one nested query. Consider the query:

> **SELECT** user_id
> **FROM** LOAN
> **WHERE** date_ret **IS NULL**;

This gives us the list of user IDs we need:

> 100
> 250
> 400

We can now specify and execute the query:

> **SELECT** name, age
> **FROM** PATRON
> **WHERE** user_id **IN** (100,250,400);

Result:	name	age
	Wong	22
	Das	67
	Jones	41

These two queries can easily be combined; we replace the list *(100,250,400)* with the first subquery:

> **SELECT** name, age
> **FROM** PATRON
> **WHERE** user_id **IN**
>   (**SELECT** user_id **FROM** LOAN
>   **WHERE** date_ret **IS NULL**);

Example 3.35   List names of patrons who have borrowed a computing or history book.

> **SELECT** name
> **FROM** PATRON
> **WHERE** user_id **IN**
>   (**SELECT** user_id **FROM** LOAN
>   **WHERE** call_no **IN**
>   (**SELECT** call_no **FROM** BOOK
>   **WHERE** subject **IN**
>   ('History','Computing')));

Result:	name
	Wong
	King
	Das

Let's analyze the above **SELECT**; it is composed of three queries. The inner query is a simple one and we can consider it separately. That is, we can consider that the database system replaces it by a list of call numbers that have been retrieved from the BOOK table. The middle query retrieves user IDs of those persons who have borrowed books in the *Computing* or *History* categories. The outer query lists the names of these people.

3.11.2   Simple comparison operators: =, <, >, < =, > =

Two examples are used to illustrate the use of the comparison operators with subqueries. To the beginning SQL user, the need for subqueries in these cases is not obvious.

Example 3.36   Who has paid the largest fine?

This is such a simple question, but unfortunately, it is not easy to formulate the correct SQL query. One may be first tempted to express the query as

> **SELECT** user_id, **MAX**(fine)
> **FROM** LOAN;

However, this is *not correct.* **MAX** is a function which operates on the whole table; hence it is single-valued. There are multiple values, one for each row, of the field *user_id*; hence it is multi-valued. These two types of expressions *cannot* be mixed.

To explain the correct formulation of the query, we begin by constructing the query in two parts. First (and this corresponds to the innermost query we shall use) we find the largest fine:

> **SELECT MAX**(fine)
> **FROM** LOAN;

Result: **max(fine)**

                 36.50

This query becomes nested; each fine now needs to be compared to this maximum value:

> **SELECT** user_id
> **FROM** LOAN
> **WHERE** fine =   (SELECT MAX(fine)
>   FROM LOAN);

Result: **user_id**

                 250

The equal sign (=) is permitted for testing the subquery, since it is known that the subquery will return only one value.

Example 3.37 What is the name of the oldest patron?

> **SELECT** name
> **FROM** PATRON
> **WHERE** age = (**SELECT MAX**(age) **FROM** PATRON);

Result: **name**

Smith

3.11.3 Correlated Subqueries

The previous subqueries have been simple in that there was no "interaction" between rows of the outer table and rows of the inner table.

Example 3.38   List the names of patrons who have borrowed more than two books.

The relevant rows of the LOAN table must be accessed for each patron in the PATRON table to determine how many books each patron has borrowed.

```
SELECT name
FROM PATRON
WHERE 3 < =        (SELECT COUNT(*)
                   FROM LOAN
                   WHERE loan.user_id
                   = patron.user_id);
```

Result: **name**

King

Think of the subquery as being executed once for each row of PATRON. For each row of PATRON, the loan table is accessed and a count is made of the number of rows retrieved. If 3 is less than or equal to that count, the patron's name will be listed.

3.11.4 Testing for existence

Sometimes one is only concerned with whether or not a subquery retrieves any rows. The **EXISTS** operator evaluates to *True* when a subquery retrieves at least one row, and *False* when a subquery retrieves no rows.

Example 3.39   Which titles have been borrowed by patrons?

SELECT title
FROM BOOK
WHERE EXISTS
            (**SELECT** *
            FROM LOAN
            WHERE loan.call_no = book.call_no);

Result: **title**

                    Physics Handbook
                    Modula-2
                    Database Design
                    Software Testing
                    Business Society
                    Graphs
                    Cell Biology
                    Set Theory

In this example, a book title is listed only when the subquery retrieves one or more rows. Note that *Database Systems* is not listed. To list the books which have not been borrowed at all, replace **EXISTS** with **NOT EXISTS**.

3.11.5   Use of ALL, ANY

ANY and **ALL** can easily lead to difficulties and so we have left them till last. The comparison operators (=, <, >, < >, < =, > =) can be used with **ANY** or **ALL** to test a specific value against a list of values. The following outlines alternative approaches and operators.

original	*alternative*
= ANY	IN
< > ANY	NOT IN
> = ALL	= . . . max (. . .) . . .
< = ALL	= . . . min.(. . .) . . .

Example 3.40   Determine the name of the oldest library patron.

This was done previously in example 3.37. Using "> = **ALL**", we can reformulate the query as

> **SELECT** name
> **FROM** PATRON
> **WHERE** age > = **ALL**
>   (**SELECT** age **FROM** PATRON);

We consider example 3.37 to be a clearer statement, and, in general, we suggest the use of the above alternatives to **ALL** and **ANY**.

3.12   Set Operations: UNION, DIFFERENCE, AND INTERSECTION

Some SQL implementations include

- **UNION**   to *combine* the results of two **SELECT**s;

- **DIFFERENCE** or **MINUS**   to *subtract* one result from another; and

- **INTERSECTION**   to determine the rows *in common* for two results.

These operators require their operands to be **UNION** compatible: the columns of one **SELECT** must agree in number and in type with the columns of the other **SELECT**.

UNION

The results of two **SELECTS** can be combined using **UNION**.

Example 3.41   List the call numbers of books borrowed by user 200, and users with IDs larger than 300.

SELECT call_no
FROM LOAN
WHERE user_id = 200

UNION

SELECT call_no
FROM LOAN
WHERE user_id > 300;

The result of the above is the *combination* of two sets—the union of the result of the two **SELECTS**s:

Result:	call_id
	900
	400
	600
	800

Only two **SELECTS**s are combined in the above; SQL permits any number of **SELECTS**s to be combined using **UNION**. Note that redundant rows in the result were eliminated. If this is not desired, **UNION ALL** should be specified instead of **UNION**.

DIFFERENCE

Example 3.42   Determine which *Computing* books have not been borrowed from the library.

One way to approach this is to use two **SELECTS**s. The first query would retrieve the call numbers of *Computing* books from the BOOK table. The second query would retrieve the call numbers of books in the LOAN table. If we *subtract* the results of the second query from the results of the first query, we will be left with the books retrieved by the first **SELECT** which were not retrieved by the second **SELECT**.

SELECT call_no
FROM BOOK
WHERE subject = 'Computing'
MINUS
SELECT call_no
FROM LOAN;

Result: **call_no**

                  200

INTERSECTION

Example 3.43   Determine which computing books have been borrowed.

We can proceed as above using two **SELECTs**, but now we want to determine what rows (call numbers) the two queries have in common:

SELECT call_no
FROM BOOK
WHERE subject = 'Computing'
INTERSECT
SELECT call_no
FROM LOAN;

Result: **call_no**

                  300
                  400
                  500

Exercises

The questions in this exercise are based on the *International Bank* case study described in Appendix A.

Simple queries

3.1 List all the customers of International Bank.

3.2 List only the customers' name and credit rating.

3.3 List all the account IDs and their credit limits.

3.4 List all bank customer transactions.

Conditional Queries

3.5 Identify all customers that have a credit limit greater than or equal to $5000.

3.6 Retrieve transactions that have occurred after 12-DEC-89.

3.7 What is the current balance of ID 100?

3.8 List all customers who have made a deposit.

3.9 Identify customers who have written a check of $1000 or more.

3.10 List all customers who have a current balance greater than $5000, but less than $50,000.

Misc. Queries

3.11 List all the cities (i.e., addresses) that have International Bank customers.

3.12 For each account number, list the number of transactions that occurred in 1988.

3.13 Retrieve the ID of the customer who has the highest current balance in the bank.

3.14 Retrieve the ID of the customer who has the lowest current balance in the bank.

3.15 List the transactions of customers whose ID is either 100, 102, 103, or 108.

3.16 How many customers does the bank have?

3.17 List customers in alphabetical order by last name.

3.18 List customers by address and, within each address, order them by name.

3.19 How many customers are there with *excellent* credit rating?

3.20 For each credit rating category (i.e., *excellent, good, poor*), list the number of customers in that category.

Joins

3.21 List the ID, name and current balance for all customers at the bank.

3.22 List the name and credit limit for all customers at the bank.

3.23 List the names of all customers who have a current balance greater than $4000.

3.24 List the ID, account number and amount of transaction (deposit withdrawal) for all customers.

3.25 For all transactions, list customer name, ID, account, date and amount.

3.26 For all transactions that took place on 05-Aug-89, list customer name, ID, account number, date and amount of transaction.

3.27 List the accounts that have not been active.

3.28 List all transactions that are greater than the average transaction amount.

3.29 List the ID and name of all bank customers that have either a *poor* rating or a negative current balance, or both.

3.30 List the name and ID of customers who have a negative current balance but do not have a *poor* credit rating.

3.31 Assume that a customer can have several credit ratings (such as *good, excellent*). List all customers at the bank that have the same credit ratings as customer ID 101.

3.32 List the new current balance for all customers; display the ID, account number, and name.

4

Data Manipulation:
Updating the Database

In this chapter we introduce Data Manipulation Language statements responsible for updating the database.

There are three commands for updating:

- **UPDATE** — to modify rows of tables
- **DELETE** — to remove rows from tables
- **INSERT** — to add new rows to tables

4.1 Modifying Rows

The general form of the **UPDATE** command is

    UPDATE table
    SET field-assignments
    WHERE condition

The *field-assignments* are of the form "*field = expression*" and are used to assign specific values to the fields of a row. The expressions must be appropriate for the data type of the corresponding column. These expressions cannot be subqueries, or involve aggregate operators such as (**AVG, COUNT,** etc.) The **WHERE** clause is optional; if it is absent, the **UPDATE** applies to all rows.

Example 4.1 Increase every patron's age by 10 years.

UPDATE PATRON
SET age = age + 10;

Result: Before Increase

user_id	name	age
100	Wong	22
150	Colin	31
200	King	21
250	Das	67
300	Niall	17
350	Smith	72
400	Jones	41

After increase

user_id	name	age
100	Wong	32
150	Colin	41
200	King	31
250	Das	77
300	Niall	27
350	Smith	82
400	Jones	51

Note that every row of PATRON is modified since there is no **WHERE** clause. Each row of PATRON is modified according to the field assignments. There is only one field assignment; *age = age +* 10. The effect of this is to cause the current value of *age* in a row to be increased by 10; the value of this expression becomes the new value of the *age* field for the row.

Example 4.2 Determine fines for books at the rate of ten cents a day.

In this example we want to modify only those rows of LOAN which meet the criteria:

- the fine field is currently null,
- the book has been returned,
- the book was overdue

```
UPDATE LOAN
SET fine = (date_ret — date_due) * 0.10
WHERE fine IS NULL
AND date_ret > date_due;
```

Result: Before Update

call_no	user_id	date due	date_ret	fine	paid
100	100	12-SEP-88	01-SEP-88		
300	100	01-SEP-88			
900	200	01-SEP-88	20-DEC-88		
400	200	04-DEC-89	16-MAY-90		
600	200	04-DEC-89	16-MAY-90		
500	250	02-OCT-84			
600	250	02-OCT-84	02-OCT-85		
700	300	10-DEC-88	01-DEC-88		
800	350	01-DEC-88	30-DEC-88		
900	400	01-OCT-90			

After Update

call_no	user_id	date_due	date_ret	fine	paid
100	100	12-SEP-88	01-SEP-88		
300	100	01-SEP-88			
900	200	01-SEP-88	20-DEC-88	1.90	
400	200	04-DEC-89	16-MAY-90	16.30	
600	200	04-DEC-89	16-MAY-90	16.30	
500	250	02-OCT-84			
600	250	02-OCT-84	02-OCT-85	36.50	
700	300	10-DEC-88	01-DEC-88		
800	350	01-DEC-88	30-DEC-88	2.90	
900	400	01-OCT-90			

4.2 Deleting Rows

The general form of the **DELETE** command is

>**DELETE**
>**FROM** table
>**WHERE** condition;

The effect of **DELETE** is the removal of rows from the table; the rows deleted are those that satisfy the condition specified in the **WHERE** clause. The **WHERE** clause is optional; if it is absent, all rows are deleted.

Example 4.3 Remove *Computing* books from the database.

>**DELETE FROM** BOOK
>**WHERE** subject = 'Computing';

Result: **Before Deletion**

call_no	title	subject
100	Physics Handbook	Physics
200	Database Systems	Computing
300	Modula-2	Computing
400	Database Design	Computing
500	Software Testing	Computing
600	Business Society	Business
700	Graphs	Mathematics
800	Cell Biology	Biology
900	Set Theory	Mathematics

After Deletion

call_no	title	subject
100	Physics Handbook	Physics
600	Business Society	Business
700	Graphs	Mathematics
800	Cell Biology	Biology
900	Set Theory	Mathematics

Example 4.4   Remove all loan records for patron *King.*

DELETE FROM LOAN
  WHERE user_id = (**SELECT** user_id.
                FROM PATRON
                WHERE name = 'King');

Result: **Before Delete**

call_no	user_id	date_due	date_ret	fine	paid
100	100	12-SEP-88	01-SEP-88		
300	100	01-SEP-88			
900	200	01 SEP 88	20 DEC 88	1.90	
400	200	04-DEC-89	16-MAY-90	16.30	
600	200	04-DEC-89	16-MAY-90	16.30	
500	250	02-OCT-84			
600	250	02-OCT-84	02-OCT-85	36.50	
700	300	10-DEC-88	01-DEC-88		
800	350	01-DEC-88	30-DEC-88	2.90	
900	400	01-OCT-90			

After Delete

call_no	user_id	date_due	date_ret	fine	paid
100	100	12-SEP-88	01-SEP-88		
300	100	01-SEP-88			
500	250	02-OCT-84			
600	250	02-OCT-84	02-OCT-85	36.50	
700	300	10-DEC-88	01-DEC-88		
800	350	01-DEC-88	30-DEC-88	2.90	
900	400	01-OCT-90			

As illustrated, subqueries can be used.

4.3   Inserting New Rows

In this section, we illustrate how new rows are inserted in a table. There are two forms of the **INSERT** command

a) **INSERT**
   INTO table (field-list)
   VALUES (constant, constant, . . .);

b) **INSERT**
   INTO table (field-list)
   subquery;

The first form is used to insert a single row; the second form is used to insert multiple rows that come from one or more existing tables. If all fields are included and the values are given in order, the field list can be omitted. Example 4.5 illustrates how one row is added to a database.

Example 4.5 Add a new patron to the database.

INSERT INTO PATRON (user_id, name, age)
VALUES (900, 'Dattani', 20);

Result:	user_id	name	age
	100	Wong	32
	150	Colin	41
	200	King	31
	250	Das	77
	300	Niall	27
	350	Smith	82
	400	Jones	51
	. . .		
	. . .		
	. . .		
	900	Dattani	20

This method is clumsy—some other approach is needed to add several rows to a table. SQL systems typically provide a forms-based interface or a load utility to enter many rows or to load a database. These facilities are discussed in later chapters dealing with DB2, ORACLE and dBASE.

The second form for **INSERT** is illustrated next.

Example 4.6   Create a table of senior citizens.

```
CREATE TABLE SENIORS
        (user_id NUMERIC          NOT NULL,
            name CHARACTER(30)  NOT NULL);

INSERT INTO SENIORS
        SELECT user_id, name
        FROM PATRON
        WHERE age > = 65;
```

Exercises

The questions in this exercise are based on the *International Bank* case study described in Appendix A.

4.1   Change the credit ratings of all customers with credit ratings of *good* to credit ratings to *v.good.*

4.2   Delete from the customer table all customers who have a *bad* credit rating.

4.3   Delete all references to the above record from the database.

4.4   Delete the account number *105* and its associated transactions from all tables.

4.5   Consider the various transactions made by account number *01111* and update the balance.

4.6   Change the name of the customer *Burns* to *Richie.*

4.7   Consider the various transactions made by all customers and update the current balance in the account table.

4.8   Create a new table called AFFLUENT compatible with the CUSTOMER table. Insert only customers with *excellent* ratings into this table. The rows should be stored sorted by name.

5

Views

All of our discussions to this point have dealt with tables. Views are similar to tables; in many cases they can be used interchangeably. A view is defined using the **CREATE VIEW** command and is defined in terms of tables or other views. A view exists in definition only: it does not occupy space in the database as a table does, but is materialized by the database system whenever it is used or referenced. There are two reasons for using views: convenience and security.

5.1 Creating Views

The **CREATE VIEW** command is used to create a view; it has the syntax:

> **CREATE VIEW** view-name (column-specification-list)
> **AS** select-specification
> **WITH CHECK OPTION;**

The *column-specification-list* is the list of columns that appear in the view. It can be omitted when each column in the view is derived directly and unambiguously from a column of an underlying table. The *select-specification* is the **SELECT** statement which defines the view. The **WITH CHECK OPTION** is optional and is concerned with security aspects of the view.

For example, to supply our patrons with a *view* of the LOAN table consisting of the *call number* and *date due* columns for those books that are currently out on loan, define the view OUT_BOOKS:

```
CREATE VIEW OUT_BOOKS
AS      SELECT call_no, date_due
        FROM LOAN
        WHERE date_ret IS NULL;
```

The **SELECT** statement is straightforward: it retrieves all rows of LOAN where the *date returned* field has not been assigned a value (books that are still out on loan). The definition of the view specifies just two columns: *call number* and *date ret.* The execution of the **CREATE VIEW** causes the system to save this definition, permitting patrons to reference OUT_BOOKS later on just as they reference tables. Thus a patron could now enter a command such as

```
SELECT * FROM OUT_BOOKS
WHERE call_no = 100;
```

to determine if the book with call number 100 is currently out on loan and when the book may be returned. By using OUT_BOOKS, the **SELECT** is simpler to code and the user does not *see* irrelevant columns. In this case, the phrase *"date_due IS NULL"* does not have to be included in the **WHERE** clause, nor will user IDs be seen in the result.

5.2 Dropping Views

ANSI SQL does not include a command to drop (remove) a view, but SQL systems generally include a **DROP** statement for this purpose. So, to remove the view OUT_BOOKS from the system one would execute:

```
DROP VIEW OUT_BOOKS;
```

5.3 Security

The view mechanism of SQL is a very useful tool for providing security in the database system. A view represents a subset of underlying tables. The user's perception is simplified, and what may be sensitive data is excluded. For example, it may be undesirable for people to know who has the book they want. If somehow we can force users to use OUT_BOOKS instead of LOAN then we have excluded (hidden) from them the sensitive field *user_id* in LOAN.

5.3.1 System variable USER

In our discussion of the **SELECT** statement, we discussed the use of system variables. One system variable of interest here is **USER**. **USER** always contains the system identifier of the person who references it, and, of course, no two people would have the same value for the variable **USER**; it is a unique identifier. When people *log-on* to the database system, they identify themselves with their system identifiers.

We can make special use of the system identifier to provide security for sensitive data. Suppose that the *user_i*d for library patrons is the same as their system identifier. Further, let us allow patrons to make inquiries regarding the information in the PA-TRON table, but not to view another patron's data. Consider the following:

> **CREATE VIEW** USER_INQUIRY **AS**
>   **SELECT** user_id, name, age
>   **FROM** PATRON **WHERE** user_id = **USER**;
>
> **GRANT SELECT ON** user_inquiry **TO PUBLIC;**

We have granted access to this view to all users of the database system (see chapter 7). However, the information is restricted according to the patron's system identifier.

5.4 Grouped Views

A *grouped* view is one where the **GROUP BY** clause has been used in the definition. Such views are very useful, but unfortunately they are subject to numerous restrictions in ANSI SQL. Consider the view:

```
CREATE VIEW LOANS_BY_BOOK (call_no, book_count)
AS
        SELECT call_no, COUNT(*)
        FROM LOAN
        GROUP BY call_no;
```

ANSI SQL does not allow one to use a **WHERE** clause, a **GROUP BY** clause, or a **HAVING** clause when a grouped view is referenced by a **SELECT**. For example,

```
SELECT * FROM LOANS_BY_BOOK
WHERE book_count > 2;
```

is not acceptable since the **SELECT** references a grouped view and contains a **WHERE** clause on that view. In addition, if one of the tables/views in the **FROM** clause of a **SELECT** references a grouped view, no other tables/views can be referenced. For example the syntax

```
SELECT loans_by_book.call_no, title
FROM LOANS_BY_BOOK, BOOK
WHERE loans_by_book.call_no = book.call_no;
```

is illegal since there are two tables/views in the **FROM** clause, and one of these is a grouped view. If a **SELECT** command references a grouped view in its **FROM** clause, an associated **WHERE**, **GROUP BY**, or **HAVING** clause is not permitted. Some SQL implementations, however, are more liberal in their treatment of grouped views.

5.5 CHECK Option

The **WITH CHECK OPTION** phrase is optional, but certainly recommended if the view could be used for updating the database. Regardless of whether or not the **WITH CHECK OPTION** is specified, the user of a view is restricted to retrieving only that portion of the database specified in the view's creation. However, that is not the case for the update operations of **INSERT** and **UPDATE**. Consider the view:

```
CREATE VIEW COMPUTING_BOOKS
AS
    SELECT * FROM BOOK
    WHERE subject = 'Computing';
```

A SELECT command referencing this view can only access *computing* books, but it is possible in the absence of **WITH CHECK OPTION**, to insert non-computing books into the database:

```
INSERT INTO COMPUTING_BOOKS
VALUES
(111, 'Twentieth Century', 'History');
```

This book, however, will suddenly *vanish* from the view; we cannot retrieve it using COMPUTING_BOOKS. A similar situation exists for the **UPDATE** command. To avoid this kind of behavior, we just include **WITH CHECK OPTION** when we define the view. This option tells the system to check and reject updates (**INSERT**s and **UPDATE**s) for rows which would vanish from the view.

5.6 Updating through Views

Some views are inherently non-updatable; an update on some views does not make any sense and must be disallowed. For example, consider the update operation

```
UPDATE LOANS_BY_BOOK
SET book_count = 25
WHERE call_no = 100;
```

Updating the *book_count* field does not make any sense; it doesn't even correspond to a field in an underlying real table. Which views can sensibly be updated and which cannot, is an area of current research in database systems. Consequently, SQL systems are quite restrictive on the types of views that can be updated. In general, a view is updatable if it corresponds to a simple row and column subset of a single table. The specific conditions that an updatable view must meet are:

- The **FROM** clause specifies exactly one table.
- The columns are derived directly from underlying columns: no arithmetic expressions, no aggregate functions, no **DISTINCT** specifications.
- The **WHERE** clause does not have a subquery, a **GROUP BY** clause, or a **HAVING** clause.

In the future, it is likely that these restrictions will be relaxed; some database systems have already eased them. For instance, DB2 allows a view to be updated even if the **WHERE** clause contains a subquery, as long as the **FROM** clause in the subquery and the outer **FROM** clause reference different tables.

Exercises

The questions in this exercise are based on the *International Bank* case study *described* in Appendix A.

5.1 Create a view called BALANCE from the International Bank database that consists of customer name, account number and current balance.

5.2 Remove the view BALANCE.

5.3 Define a view called CREDIT_RATING that consists of ID, name, credit rating, and account number.

5.4 What does the **CHECK OPTION** syntax in SQL refer to?

5.5 What are grouped views?

5.6 Can we update a database using views? Explain.

6
Integrity

Integrity in a database is concerned with the database having correct and consistent data. There are two basic integrity constraints that are considered part of the relational model. These are *primary key integrity* and *referential integrity*. Primary key integrity is concerned with the values that primary keys assume, and referential integrity is concerned with inter-table references.

Neither primary key nor referential integrity are included in ANSI SQL. However, the importance of integrity is well known, and the initial proposals for SQL included a general-purpose construct, the **ASSERT** statement, for declaring integrity constraints. Relational database systems that provide integrity capabilities are appearing. In the discussion which follows, we will be using DB2 as an example; in 1988, DB2 began providing support for referential integrity.

6.1 Primary Key Integrity

A *primary key* is a field, or combination of fields, that uniquely identify rows in a table. For example, every book of the library is assigned a unique call number. Hence, the *call_no* field is the primary key for the BOOK table.

The constraint for primary keys is defined as

no field constituting part of a primary key may be null

The implications of this rule should seem clear. If this rule is enforced, every primary key value will uniquely and completely identify some row in a table. With respect to our BOOK table, it means that each row (each book) can be unambiguously identified. There is at most one row in BOOK for any given call number.

We give examples of defining the library database including the definition of primary keys.

```
CREATE TABLE BOOK (
    PRIMARY KEY(call_no),
    call_no       NUMERIC           NOT NULL,
    title         CHARACTER(30)     NOT NULL,
    subject       CHARACTER(12));

CREATE TABLE PATRON (
    PRIMARY KEY (user_id),
    user_id       NUMERIC           NOT NULL,
    name          CHARACTER(30)     NOT NULL,
    age           NUMERIC);

CREATE TABLE LOAN (
    PRIMARY KEY (call_no, user_id, date_due),
    call no        NUMERIC           NOT NULL,
    user_id        NUMERIC           NOT NULL,
    data_due       DATE              NOT NULL,
    date_ret       DATE,
    fine           MONEY);
```

The choices of *call_no* and *user_id* as primary keys for the BOOK and PATRON tables are quite reasonable. Our choice of primary key for the LOAN table will work for our small database, but would not be acceptable in practice. It would prevent someone from borrowing the same book twice on the same day.

With DB2, each table can optionally have at most one primary key. Note that a primary key may be composite; the primary key for the LOAN table is made up of three fields. Two other restrictions apply:

- each field in a primary key must be declared **NOT NULL**
- each table must have a unique index created for the primary key.

Note that any table could have more than one unique identifier; that is, more than one *key*. For example, if the BOOK table included the ISBN, it also would be a unique identifier. However, for any one table we usually designate one key as the primary key.

Up to this point, it seems that the **PRIMARY KEY** clause is merely descriptive: the effect of a primary key is made possible by the **NOT NULL** attribute and the unique index, not by the **PRIMARY KEY** clause. This clause, however, is required for the enforcement of referential integrity, which is discussed next.

6.2 Referential Integrity

Consider our library database.

BOOK:	call_no, title, subject
LOAN:	call_no, user_id, date_due, date_ret, fine
PATRON:	user_id, name, age

We have underlined the primary keys; this is standard convention. There are some connections between the tables that concern primary keys used in many of our queries. The *call_no* and *user_id* fields in the LOAN table are actually references to books in the BOOK table and patrons in the PATRON table. These two fields in the LOAN table are two examples of *foreign keys*. In our database there are two constraints we expect to hold:

1. Each *call_no* in the LOAN table matches a *call_no* in the BOOK table, and

2. Each *user_id* in the LOAN table matches a *user_id* in the PATRON table.

These constraints are examples of *foreign key integrity constraints*. A *foreign key* is a field (or combination of fields) in one table that corresponds to the primary key of another table. By *referential integrity* we mean each value a foreign key assumes must either be

- null, or
- equal to a value of the primary key in the referenced table.

These rules prevent a situation in which a row of LOAN specifies a patron or book that does not exist in the other tables.

DB2 uses the terms *parent* and *dependent* to specify the role that tables play in referential integrity. The referenced table (BOOK, for example) is referred to as the parent, and the referencing table (LOAN, for example) is referred to as the *dependent.*

Also, a row such as:

call_no	title	subject
900	Set Theory	Mathematics

in the BOOK table is a parent row for the following rows in LOAN:

call_no	user_id	date_due	date_ret	fine	paid
900	200	01-SEP-88	20-DEC-88	1.90	yes
900	400	01-OCT-90			

Note that each of these rows in the LOAN table have different parent rows in the PATRON table (patrons *200* and *400*).

Referential integrity is very important to the users of database systems (we need correct and consistent data if we are to rely on the database), and we certainly expect to see more implementations in the near future. If a system does not implement referential integrity, then its users must ensure that integrity remains intact as the database is updated. To do so means that the users (or programmers, or application programs) must execute appropriate SQL commands.

DB2's implementation of referential integrity requires the specification of delete and update rules in the **CREATE TABLE** command. For each foreign key in a table, the database designer must specify the appropriate action to be taken by the system whenever a pertinent deletion or update takes place. We discuss these rules next.

6.3 Rules for Referential Integrity

When a table is created using **CREATE TABLE**, integrity rules and related clauses may be included. DB2 allows one to specify primary keys, foreign keys, delete rules, and update rules in the **CREATE TABLE** command. For each foreign key, a delete rule and an update rule is given. These rules govern the actions taken by the system when an attempt is made to delete or update a referenced primary key value. There are no options regarding insertion or updating of foreign key values; we discuss implicit rules for this case.

DELETE rule

A delete rule is given for each foreign key in a table. The rule specifies the action the database system must take if a parent row is deleted. The possible actions are:

action	effect
• **RESTRICT**	The deletion of a parent row will be disallowed if there are any dependent rows.
• **CASCADE**	If a parent row is deleted, then the system will automatically delete the dependent rows.
• **SET NULL**	When a parent row is deleted, all dependent foreign keys are set to NULL.

We shall discuss each of these options and its effect on the library database. For example, what action would be appropriate if a book is deleted (suppose the book is taken out of circulation because it was lost or outdated)? The database designer must anticipate these situations and determine an appropriate action.

RESTRICT option

Suppose the database designer considers that books should not be deleted from the database if there are any records that reference that book. To have this decision automatically enforced by the system, the designer might define the LOAN table as

```
CREATE TABLE LOAN (
        PRIMARY KEY(call_no, user_id, date_due),
        FOREIGN KEY (call_no)
                        REFERENCES BOOK
                        ON DELETE RESTRICT,
        call_no       NUMERIC      NOT NULL,
        user_id       NUMERIC      NOT NULL,
        date_due      DATE         NOT NULL,
        date_ret      DATE,
        fine          MONEY,
        paid          CHAR(3));
```

There are two rows in LOAN which have call number equal to 900. Therefore, a delete for the book *Set Theory* (call number 900) would not be allowed, since dependents exist for it.

CASCADE option

Suppose the database designer considers the following action as the appropriate one:

If a book is deleted, all loan records for that book must also be deleted.

If our database is to reflect activity for current books and current patrons, the above action is reasonable. The LOAN table would then be defined as

```
CREATE TABLE LOAN (
        PRIMARY KEY(call_no, user_id, date_due),
        FOREIGN KEY (call_no)
                        REFERENCES book
                        ON DELETE CASCADE,
        call_no       NUMERIC           NOT NULL,
        user_id       NUMERIC           NOT NULL,
        date_due      DATE              NOT NULL,
        date_ret      DATE,
        fine          MONEY,
        paid          CHAR(3));
```

If we attempted to delete the book *Set Theory*, it would be successful. However, due to the **CASCADE** clause for the LOAN table (which references the BOOK table), corresponding dependents in LOAN would also be deleted. That is, the deletion propagates to the LOAN table, and, in our example, two rows of LOAN are deleted by the system. The deletion of the dependent rows is a side-effect that is transparent to the user who deletes the parent row.

SET NULL option

Suppose the database designer considers the following action as the appropriate one:

If a book is deleted, then all loan records that reference that book must have the call number set to NULL.

The designer has chosen that deletions of parents should be unhindered, and that all references to such a deleted row should be nullified. This may be an appropriate choice if there is a need to keep track of all fines paid by the library patrons even after the referenced books have long disappeared. The LOAN table would be defined as

```
CREATE TABLE LOAN (
        FOREIGN KEY (call_no)
                REFERENCES BOOK
                ON DELETE SET NULL,
    call_no        NUMERIC,
    user_id        NUMERIC        NOT NULL,
    date_due       DATE           NOT NULL,
    date_ret       DATE,
    fine           MONEY,
    paid           CHAR(3));
```

For this example to work, it was necessary to omit the primary key specification for the LOAN table. For our database, the foreign keys also happen to be part of a primary key and so could not be NULL. (This is certainly not always the case; we shall give another example later on.) Therefore, if one deletes the book *Set Theory*, the pertinent rows of LOAN are also updated. Once again, this is transparent to the user and is done by the system. The result is:

call_no	user_id	date_due	date_ret	fine	paid
	200	01-SEP-88	20-DEC-88	1.90	yes
	400	01-OCT-90			

where the call number field is now NULL.

It is common for foreign keys to be separate from a primary key. As a simple example consider a DEPARTMENT table and an EMPLOYEE table.

> DEPARTMENT: *dept_no*, dept_name, manager
> EMPLOYEE: *staff_id*, name, dept_no

An employee row could have a department field (*dept_no*) which references the DEPARTMENT table, but the primary key for the EMPLOYEE table could be a field such as *staff_id*. With this database, it would be possible to have primary keys for both tables, and the EMPLOYEE table could specify **SET NULL** for the foreign key *dept_no*.

UPDATE rules

For each foreign key, an update rule is given. This specifies the action to be undertaken by the system when a primary key is updated. As with **DELETE** rules, there are three options: **RESTRICT**, **CASCADE**, and **SET NULL**. We outline the actions taken by the system.

action	effect

- **RESTRICT**   If an **UPDATE** command changes the primary key of a parent row and if dependents exist for that row, the **UPDATE** is disallowed.

- **CASCADE**   If an **UPDATE** command changes the primary key of a parent row, all of its dependent rows will have their foreign key updated to the same value.

- **SET NULL**   When an **UPDATE** command changes the primary key of a parent row, all of its dependent rows will have their foreign key set to **NULL**.

These actions are very similar to that for the **DELETE** rule. At the time of writing, however, DB2 only supports the **RESTRICT** action for **UPDATE**. Hence, the **UPDATE** rules for LOAN could be defined as

```
CREATE TABLE LOAN (
        PRIMARY KEY(call_no, user_id, date_due),
        FOREIGN KEY (call_no)
                        REFERENCES BOOK
                        ON UPDATE RESTRICT,
        FOREIGN KEY (user_id)
                        REFERENCES PATRON
                        ON UPDATE RESTRICT,
        call_no         NUMERIC         NOT NULL,
        user_id         NUMERIC         NOT NULL,
        date_due        DATE            NOT NULL,
        date_ret        DATE,
        fine            MONEY,
        paid            CHAR(3));
```

Implicit INSERT and UPDATE rules for foreign key values

In a sense, there are implicit rules utilized by the system whenever *foreign keys* are updated or inserted. The system handles these in a standard way: the parent row for a foreign key value must already exist, or else the **UPDATE** or **INSERT** is disallowed. This is merely the enforcement of the referential integrity rule itself.

6.4 Primary Key Restrictions and Misc. Details

We have discussed primary key and referential integrity. From this the reader should obtain an understanding of the principles involved. The subject is somewhat more complex than our coverage here. There are further restrictions and details that we have excluded. We list some of these here.

- When a primary key is updated, the update must be a singleton update. That is, the update statement must reference just a single row of the table.
- A primary key cannot be updated via a cursor.
- If a table is both the parent and the dependent for a constraint, then the **DELETE** rule must be a **CASCADE**.

The implementation of primary and referential integrity are useful additions to a database system. Data integrity is of concern to the database designer, analyst, and user.

Exercises

The questions in this exercise are based on the *International Bank* case study described in Appendix A.

6.1 Customer *Kent* has decided to close his account at the bank. Delete all relevant rows. Write SQL code, assuming that your system

a) supports referential integrity

b) does not support referential integrity

6.2 Assuming that your system does not support referential integrity, how will you detect violations?

6.3 Assuming that your system does not support referential integrity, what code will implement

a) the cascade rule for update?

b) the restrict rule for delete?

7

Database System Management

This chapter describes various aspects of SQL that are related to database administration and management. Four special topics are presented here — indexing controlling access to data, concurrency control and recovery, and system catalogs.

7.1 Indexes

Indexes are not specified in ANSI SQL, but commercial SQL systems allow the user to establish them to improve performance. The presence of an index does not affect what one can or cannot specify when retrieving or updating the database. In fact, a user of a SQL database does not have to be aware of the existence of indexes.

An index is based on one or more columns of a table. Their purpose is to permit direct and efficient access to rows of a table when a query has specified values for the columns on which the index is based. As an analogy, the index at the end of this book permits *direct access* to pages containing information on a certain topic.

Consider the LOAN table. If someone retrieves the loan information for *user_id* 100, then the row(s) will be retrieved regardless of whether or not an index (on *user_id*) exists. If, however, there is no index on *user_id*, then the database system must scan the entire table for those rows with the value *100* in the *user_id* column. This means that the system must retrieve the whole table and, if there are many rows, this will be time-consuming. If such queries are anticipated and if one wants them executed as quickly as possible, one should define a *user_id* index for the LOAN table.

The **CREATE INDEX** command has the syntax:

> **CREATE INDEX** index-name   *or*
> **CREATE UNIQUE INDEX** index-name
> **ON** table-name (column-specifications);

The specification of **UNIQUE** is optional. If specified, the system will enforce uniqueness of the column values on which the index is built. A *column-specification* consists of a column name and (optionally) whether the ordering is **ASC**ending or **DESC**ending (**ASC** is the default).

Creating single-column indexes

On any table one can establish indexes on individual fields or combinations of fields. For example, to establish an index on *user-id* for the PATRON table we would execute

> **CREATE INDEX** XPATRON
> **ON PATRON** (user_id **ASC**);

When the above command is executed, the index is established and entries pertinent to existing rows in PATRON are created.

Creating concatenated indexes

A *concatenated index* is created when more than one column is enclosed in parentheses:

> **CREATE INDEX** XPATRON
> **ON** PATRON (user_id, age);

Creating UNIQUE indexes

As indicated earlier, using **UNIQUE** will cause uniqueness to be enforced by the database system. In the example below, the index will prevent duplicate *user_id*s during data entry.

CREATE UNIQUE INDEX XPATRON
ON PATRON (user_id);

DROPping Indexes

Indexes can be deleted either by removing the index or by discarding the table itself. When a table is dropped, all tables associated with the index are automatically removed. Dropping (removing) indexes, such as XPATRON is done by simply executing

DROP INDEX XPATRON;

Indexing for performance

Indexing does not help if a table with few rows in it is being used. It is only beneficial when tables are large. Moreover, since indexes are updated automatically, having too many indexes will affect response time. Performance data should be gathered before deciding if indexing is required, and a needs analysis will determine how many indexes per table should be provided.

Points to consider are:

- It is useful to index the primary key in every table.
- Indexes are maintained by the system. Each update and insertion can incur overhead for the updating of indexes.
- Loading or inserting data before creating indexes may be beneficial in terms of response time.
- Each index consumes disk space.

7.2 Data Control Language: Controlling Access to Data

ANSI SQL contains two commands for controlling user access to the database:

GRANT: grants user access privileges to fields in tables

REVOKE: removes user access privileges

These commands are only relevant in a multi-user system. When each user is assigned an identifier (a *user_id* or *logon_id*) that identifies him/her to the system. Whenever a user creates a table the *user_id* is associated with that table and he/she is said to "own" the table — he/she holds all access privileges to it.

A table is one example of a resource or object in a SQL system. Associated with each object is a set of operations that can be performed by users of the system. However, before anyone can access an object, he/she must be granted the privilege to do so. After creating a table, a user can pass privileges on to other users to permit them to operate **SELECT, UPDATE, INSERT**, and **DELETE** commands on that table.

GRANT and REVOKE

The **GRANT** command is used to give privileges and the **REVOKE** command is used to take away privileges. If user *Lib* created the three tables of the library database and wished to grant **SELECT** privilege on the BOOK table to users *Smith* and *Jones*, he would issue the command:

GRANT SELECT ON BOOK **TO** smith, jones;

SQL has a keyword, **PUBLIC** that refers to all users. To grant everyone access to the BOOK table one could specify

GRANT SELECT ON BOOK **TO PUBLIC**;

The syntax of **GRANT** and **REVOKE** are:

GRANT privileges **ON** table-list **TO** user-list;

REVOKE privileges **ON** table-list **FROM** user-list;

The keyword **ALL** is available to include all privileges. With the **UPDATE** privilege, one can specify that the access apply to specific columns. For example, if *clerk121* will be modifying subjects of books, we can grant *clerk121* specific access for that purpose:

GRANT UPDATE ON BOOK (subject) TO clerk121;

GRANT OPTION

It is possible to provide a **GRANT OPTION** to other users, so that they may in turn provide privileges to other users. Consider the example below, where *Carlson* is given the **GRANT** option.

GRANT SELECT ON BOOK TO carlson
WITH GRANT OPTION

Now that **GRANT** privileges have been given to user *Carlson*, *Carlson* in turn can grant privileges to a third user such as *Nordin*:

GRANT SELECT ON BOOK TO nordin
WITH GRANT OPTION

Nordin in turn can provide this privilege to user *Chen*:

GRANT SELECT ON BOOK TO chen
WITH GRANT OPTION

Now if *Carlson* revokes privileges of *Nordin*, this will result in users' *Chen* and *Nordin* having their privileges revoked automatically. Note that if *Chen* and *Nordin* have received **SELECT** privileges from yet another user, they will continue to have **SELECT** authority over the BOOK table.

Privileges table

Most database systems will provide a system catalog table which keeps track of who has what privileges. (Refer to chapter 11 for more details on catalog tables). For example, in DB2 a catalog table called SYSTABAUTH keeps track of the following information: *grantor, grantee, dbname, tcreator, authhowgot, dategranted, timegranted, alterauth, deleteauth, updateauth.* The above attributes are described below:

grantor Authorization ID of the user who granted the privileges

grantee ID of the user who received the privilege

dategranted Date the privileges were granted

alterauth Indicates whether or not the grantee can alter the table

deleteauth Indicates whether or not the grantee can delete rows

indexauth Indicates whether or not the grantee can index the table

updateauth Indicates whether or not the grantee can update rows of the table or view

authhowgot Indicates the authorization level of the user from whom the privileges were received; for example, *S* indicates from the *S*ystem Administrator, *D* indicates from the *D*atabase Administrator,

In the case of the attributes *alterauth, deleteauth, indexauth,* and *updateauth,* there are three possible values: a *blank* indicating that the privilege is not held, **G** indicating that privilege is held with **GRANT OPTION**, and **Y** indicating that privilege is held without **GRANT OPTION**.

7.3 Transactions: Concurrency and Recovery

A transaction is a *unit of work* in a database system. In SQL, we say a transaction is a collection of SQL commands; it may be only one command or several. Once a user has executed some commands, he can either make the changes permanent by **COMMIT**ting his work, or he can undo the changes by **ROLL**ing **BACK**. SQL provides two commands for these purposes:

COMMIT WORK;
ROLLBACK WORK;

The keyword **WORK** is optional. **COMMIT** informs the system that the current transaction is finished, and that any changes are to become permanent in the database. **ROLLBACK** instructs the system to remove any changes done by the current transaction, and make it look as though the changes were never done in the first place. When a user logs-on, he begins his first transaction. **COM-MIT**s and **ROLLBACK**s delimit transactions, and his last transaction terminates when he logs-off the system.

Transactions in a database system must have four properties: *atomicity, consistency, isolation,* and *durability.*

Atomicity means that a transaction is an all-or-nothing phenomenon. It is either done in its entirety or not at all. An excellent example comes from banking. Consider a transaction in which money is being moved from one account to another. Partial completion of this transaction would not be tolerated; it must be done completely, or (in the event of a failure) it must "look" as though it never occurred at all. To enforce this, a database system usually uses a log or journal (discussed later).

Consistency means that a transaction must preserve the correctness of the database. To achieve this, the transaction must perform only correct actions.

In a multiuser environment, many users can concurrently access the database, and the database system must ensure that users do not adversely affect one another. Transactions must be *isolated* from one another until they have been completed. Consider the banking example again. If transactions are allowed access to the same account information, their activities must be synchronized. The most common technique used by database systems to synchronize transactions is *locking.*

Transactions must be *durable.* For instance, if a transaction deposits funds to an account, that deposit should not disappear. If the database is damaged (by disk failure, for example), then the system must be able to recover and restore the database to its latest consistent state.

Logs

Typically a database system keeps a log of changes made to a database. This log could be a file on either disk or tape. Whenever a change is made to the database, information is also written in the log. Four record types that appear on logs are:

- *transaction begin*   each time a transaction starts, a record identifying the transaction and its start time is written in the log.

- *transaction end*   when a transaction executes a **COMMIT** or **ROLLBACK**, the system writes a termination message in the log.

- *before image*   the contents of a row prior to an update are written in the log.

- *after image*   the new contents of a row are written in the log.

In many database systems, the *before image* and *after image* are the keys to recovery. To **ROLLBACK** a transaction, the system accesses the relevant *before images* and restores the database from them. If the durability of a transaction is compromised, (say through a failure), the *after images* can be used to restore the database to a consistent state. In this case, restoring the database requires a prior backup copy of the database to which the *after images* can be applied. So in addition to keeping a log, the database administrator usually makes backups of the database on a regular schedule.

Concurrency controls

In a multi-user environment, it is possible that many users are accessing the database concurrently. Transactions with conflicting data requirements must be isolated to prevent them from adversely interfering with one another. The most common ways to synchronize transactions are based on locking. A simple scheme based on two types of locks is discussed.

Consider a database as consisting of resources that are things such as rows of tables, tables, indexes, and views. Whenever a user accesses a resource, he must obtain a lock on it before he may proceed. Actually the user or transaction does not explicitly request the lock; that is done by the system on his behalf. Normally, if a user is delayed, the delay will be transparent to him; he is not aware of the delay due to the speed at which processing is done. Different types of locks are used for different purposes. If a user is merely reading data, a *share lock* is required; but if a user is updating the database, an *exclusive lock* is needed.

Many share locks can be held on the same object by many users or transactions. However, only one *exclusive* lock can be held on an object. No other transactions can hold a lock on an object if some transaction holds an exclusive lock on it. It is usual for locks obtained by a transaction to be kept until the transaction terminates. This guarantees the correctness of concurrent execution, but this rule can be relaxed in some cases.

Obviously, one sees the database system's need for a *lock manager*, whose job It Is to manage the acquisition and release of locks. It must queue the transactions for which locks cannot be granted, delay them temporarily, and detect when a transaction can be resumed when its requested lock has been granted. It also must be able to detect and resolve another situation that can arise called *deadlock.*

Deadlock arises if two transactions are each waiting for each other to release a resource. Without intervention by the lock manager, these transactions would wait forever. Suppose transaction *A* is transferring funds from account X to account Y, and that another transaction *B* is transferring funds from account Y to account X. If these two transactions are executing concurrently, then *A* could acquire an exclusive lock on X, *B* acquire an exclusive lock on Y, and when each tries to acquire their next exclusive lock, each becomes deadlocked.

In most current SQL systems, when a deadlock is detected, the system picks a *victim* and issues a **ROLLBACK** on the victim's behalf. The user is then notified of the deadlock and the action taken by the system. If the user wishes, he can re-enter the transaction. Some database systems are a little more friendly: they pick a victim, roll the victim back, and then later restart the victim automatically, with no special attention required by the user (the whole affair can be totally unnoticed).

7.4 System Catalog

All SQL systems have a *catalog* — a set of *system* tables — where information about databases is kept. SQL can be used to examine this information, for it is kept in tables. These tables are mostly updated by the system through the use of commands such as **CREATE TABLE** and **CREATE VIEW**. Each commercial SQL implementation has its own names for these tables so we will use generic names:

TABLE	PURPOSE
TABLES	Gives name, owner, number of columns, etc., for each table in the database.
COLUMNS	Gives name, table, data type, etc., for each column in each table in the database.
VIEWS	Gives name, definition, owner, etc., of each view in the database.
INDEXES	Gives name of table indexed, indexed column(s), etc.

Querying the system catalog

To determine what tables are in the database, use the command

    SELECT * FROM TABLES;

To determine the columns in a table, such as TABLE, one could use

    SELECT * FROM COLUMNS
    WHERE table_name = 'table';

assuming *table name* is the correct column of COLUMNS. Systems often provide some form of *Help* utility to facilitate accessing the system catalog. It is important to realize the catalog exists and is as accessible as any other set of tables for retrieval.

Querying the catalog in DB2

This section describes how SYSTABLES is queried in DB2 (chapters 9 and 10 describe how the same is done using ORACLE and dBASE IV; chapter 11 provides additional information on the DB2 catalog). In DB2, the catalog consists of about 25 tables that are automatically updated by the system. Consequently, the creator of the tables is considered to be "SYSIBM", and all tables are prefixed with SYSIBM in the **FROM** clause.

SYSTABLES

SYSTABLES contains one row for each table and view and has attributes *tbname, creator, type, dbname, dbid, colcount, card, npages, remarks, parents, children, keycolumns, reclength. . . .*
    Some of these attributes are described below:

tbname	The name of the table or view
type	This can be **V** or **T** (view or table)
dbname	The name of the database
dbid	Internal identifier for the database
colcount	The number of columns in the table or view
card	Total number of rows in the table
npages	Total number of pages on which rows of the table appear
remarks	Provided by the user with the **COMMENT** statement
parents	The number of links in which the table is a child
children	The number of links in which the table is a parent
reclength	The maximum length of any record in the table

The use of SYSTABLES is illustrated below:

```
SELECT tbname
FROM SYSIBM.SYSTABLES
WHERE creator = 'Carlson';
```

Result: **tbname**

PATRON
BOOK
LOAN

If we wish to find out how many tables user *Carlson* has created:

SELECT COUNT(*)
FROM SYSIBM.SYSTABLES
WHERE creator = 'Carlson';

Result: count(*)

3

To determine the column count, name, and remarks for the tables created by the above user:

SELECT name, colcount, remarks
FROM SYSIBM.SYSTABLES
WHERE creator = 'Carlson'

Result: | name | colcount | remarks |
|---|---|---|
| PATRON | 3 | LIBRARY PATRONS |
| BOOK | 3 | BOOK LISTING |
| LOAN | 5 | LOAN AND FINES INFO. |

Exercises

The questions in this exercise are based on the *International Bank* case study described in Appendix A.

Indexes

7.1 Index the customers by name. Call the index XNAME.

7.2 Index all customers uniquely by ID. Call the index XID.

7.3 Create a concatenated index of customers by address and name.

7.4 Delete the XID index.

7.5 Delete the XNAME index.

Data Control Language

7.6 Write SQL statements to give *Mike* **SELECT** privileges over the entire CUSTOMER table.

7.7 Grant **SELECT** privileges to all *bank_tellers* for the CUSTOMER table.

7.8 Grant all privileges to *bank_manager* over all tables.

7.9 To all customers, provide read-only access to the TRANSACTION table.

7.10 Remove update access privileges from the *bank_tellers*.

Transactions: Concurrency and Recovery

7.11 What is a transaction?

7.12 Explain **COMMIT** and **ROLLBACK**. What significant role do they play in a transaction?

7.13 Explain how *locking* is used to solve concurrency problems.

7.14 Illustrate the explicit locking facilities of a commercial SQL System

7.15 Discuss the importance of recoverability in a database system.

7.16 What will be the impact of **ROLLBACK** if

a) you just deleted customer *Kent?*

b) if you just deleted the CUSTOMER table?

c) if you renamed *Kent* to *Frank?*

System Catalog

7.16 List all the tables in the International Bank Database.

7.17 List all the views in the database.

7.18 Obtain a list of all columns defined in the CUSTOMER table.

7.19 Provide a list of indexes in the database.

7.20 Who holds privileges on the CUSTOMER table?

8
Embedded SQL

The previous discussions have assumed that SQL was being used in an Interactive environment where someone types an SQL command at a terminal and the system sends its response back to that terminal.

In this chapter, we illustrate the use of SQL in the context of programming languages. SQL can be used with PL/I, COBOL, FORTRAN, and Pascal; various vendors permit its use with other languages as well, such as assembler, C, and ADA. ANSI SQL is *static* SQL; DB2 and other systems extend the use of SQL to allow programs to generate and execute *dynamic* SQL statements at execution time.

A program which makes use of SQL is a normal program with the inclusion of

a) SQL declarations (variables, cursors, . . .)

b) SQL statements (executions of **SELECT, UPDATE**, . . .)

that are each prefixed by the phrase EXEC SQL. The prefix enables a precompiler to process such statements replacing them, when necessary, with appropriate calls to run-time database routines. In the case of SQL, a precompiler is a program which executes prior to the compiler, and translates any SQL statements into appropriate subroutine call statements which can then be processed by the language compiler.

Each embedded SQL statement has the prefix EXEC SQL, but the terminator may vary from one language to another. We use COBOL and PL/I in our examples. For COBOL the terminator is END-EXEC, and for PL/I the terminator is a semicolon.

The SQL declarations fall into three categories:

- host variables
- exception handling
- cursor specifications

This chapter is organized as follows. We begin with *host variables* and *exception handling* followed by examples illustrating those concepts. These examples illustrate embedded SQL without *cursors*. Cursors, used when processing a query row-by-row, are discussed next. This is followed by DB2's dynamic SQL. Complete COBOL programs are given in sections 10.4 and 10.5; the PL/I equivalents appear at the end of the chapter.

8.1 Variables

ANSI SQL requires that the precompiler be notified of all host language variables that will be used within SQL statements. Host language variables are declared between the following two statements:

EXEC SQL BEGIN DECLARE SECTION

EXEC SQL END DECLARE SECTION

For example, suppose we have an application program which obtains the title and subject area for a certain book whose call number is not known until the program is executing and communicating with a user. Presumably the program obtains the specific call number from the user, retrieves the appropriate row from the database, and sends the list back to the user.

A **COBOL** program could have the WORKING-STORAGE SECTION:

```
        EXEC SQL BEGIN DECLARE SECTION END-EXEC.
01      SUBAREA PIC X(12).
01      CALLNO COMPUTATIONAL 9(4).
01      TITLE PIC X(30).
01      SQLCODE COMPUTATIONAL S9(4).
        EXEC SQL END DECLARE SECTION END-EXEC.
```

A **PL/I** program could have the following declarations:

```
        EXEC SQL BEGIN DECLARE SECTION;
        DCL SUBAREA           CHARACTER (12);
        DCL CALLNO            FIXED BIN (15);
        DCL TITLE             CHARACTER (30);
        DCL SQLCODE           FIXED BIN (31);
        EXEC SQL END DECLARE SECTION;
```

The variables SUBAREA, CALLNO, and TITLE correspond to fields of the BOOK table; SUBAREA corresponds to the column *subject*, CALLNO corresponds to the column *call_no*, and TITLE corresponds to the column *title*. To avoid ambiguities that duplicate names involve, Embedded SQL requires the programmer to prefix host language variables with a colon (:) when used within a SQL statement. The third variable defined above, SQLCODE, is required in all application programs and is introduced next.

SQLCODE

After the execution of a SQL statement, the database system returns a status code in a special variable, SQLCODE. SQLCODE is an integer and indicates if the last SQL statement was executed successfully. In many database systems, rather than being explicitly declared as shown above, a programmer uses a SQL **INCLUDE** statement to bring the definition of system variables including SQLCODE, into the program code. SQLCA stands for SQL communication area.

```
        EXEC SQL
            INCLUDE SQLCA
```

When a SQL statement has been executed, the variable SQLCODE holds the status of the database request, and this value of SQLCODE must be tested by the application program. SQLCODE is a numeric field with the following interpretation:

  0   request was successful

  100   request failed (no more rows for a **FETCH**, no data was returned by **SELECT** statement, a **DELETE** operation was unsuccessful)

  < 0   a database error was encountered (the database remains unaltered)

Other values of SQLCODE are defined in specific implementations.

NULL values

Programming languages, such as COBOL, do not utilize NULLs as SQL does. When null values are involved, an *indicator* variable is used. For example, if we obtain the fine from a specific row of the LOAN table, we detect a null value the following way:

COBOL:
```
        EXEC SQL SELECT fine
            INTO :FINE:FINEIND
            FROM LOAN
            WHERE user_id = 100
            AND call_no = 100
        END-EXEC.
*CHECK FOR A NULL VALUE
        IF FINEIND = –1 THEN . . .
```

PL/I:
```
        EXEC SQL SELECT fine
            INTO :FINE:FINEIND
            FROM LOAN
            WHERE user_id = 100
            AND call_no = 100;
/* CHECK FOR A NULL VALUE */
IF FINEIND = –1 THEN . . .
```

Note that there is no comma separating the two host variables in ":FINE:FINEIND". If the second host variable, FINEIND, has a value of –1, no value is returned for that column. This specification of a variable for null value detection can only be used in the **INTO** clause of a **SELECT** or the **SET** clause of an **UPDATE**; it cannot be specified in **WHERE** or **HAVING** clauses.

8.2 Exception Handling

Whenever a SQL statement is performed, the program must test the value of SQLCODE. Such tests are used by an application program to control its execution. A **WHENEVER** clause can be specified to inform the database system how a certain *condition* is to be handled so the application can avoid testing for that *condition.* The syntax of the **WHENEVER** clause is:

EXEC SQL WHENEVER condition action

The *conditions* are: NOT FOUND and SQLERROR. They correspond to SQLCODE being 100 or being negative respectively. (SQL implementations typically include other conditions; SQLWARNING, for example.) The action is either **CONTINUE** or a **GOTO** statement. The **GOTO** option will cause the precompiler to insert a **GOTO** statement after subsequent SQL statements that will be executed if the condition arises. **CONTINUE** (the default) means that the precompiler will not insert such tests, under the assumption that the programmer is making the appropriate tests.

The condition SQLERROR may indicate a very serious problem with the use of the database. If it ever arises, the program may need to execute a rollback to undo any work accomplished and then terminate. Using **GOTO** for SQLERROR could simplify program logic. However, the use of **CONTINUE** for NOT FOUND conditions may be appropriate for keeping the logic of the program clear; that is, to avoid the **GOTO** *type* of coding.

8.3   Operations without Cursors

In this section we describe how to retrieve single rows, how to update or delete rows, and how to insert rows without using *cursors*.

SELECT

The **SELECT**s discussed here are known as *singleton* **SELECT**s, since they retrieve a single row only. In these cases, a **SELECT** uses an **INTO** clause to specify the host variables which will receive the values of that single row.

Example 8.1   Obtain the title of the book with call number 100.
The following **SELECT**, when executed, will cause the row for book 100 to be retrieved, and the values of the *title* and *subject* fields will be placed in the host variables SUBAREA and TITLE.

```
EXEC SQL
      SELECT subject, title
      INTO :SUBAREA:SINDIC,:TITLE
            FROM BOOK WHERE call_no = 100
```

We use an indicator variable to detect a null value for the subject area.

A **COBOL** program to retrieve book 100:

```
IDENTIFICATION DIVISION.
PROGRAM-ID.      EX81.

ENVIRONMENT DIVISION.
CONFIGURATION SECTION.
DATA DIVISION.
```

```
WORKING-STORAGE SECTION.
    EXEC SQL BEGIN DECLARE SECTION END-EXEC.
01      SUBAREA         PIC X(12).
01      SINDIC          PIC S9999 COMP-5.
01      TITLE           PIC X(30).
    EXEC SQL END DECLARE SECTION END-EXEC.
    EXEC SQL INCLUDE SQLCA END-EXEC.


PROCEDURE DIVISION.
    EXEC SQL
        WHENEVER SQLERROR GOTO Z200-ERROR
    END-EXEC.

    MOVE SPACES TO TITLE, SUBAREA.

    EXEC SQL
        SELECT title, subject
        INTO :TITLE, :SUBAREA:SINDIC
        FROM BOOK
        WHERE call_no = 100
    END-EXEC.

    IF SQLCODE = 0
        IF SINDIC = -1
            DISPLAY TITLE, "**NULL**"
        ELSE DISPLAY TITLE, SUBAREA
    ELSE DISPLAY "BOOK WITH CALL_NO 100 NOT FOUND"
            DISPLAY "SQLCODE = ",SQLCODE.
    STOP RUN.

Z200-ERROR.
    DISPLAY "ERROR DISPLAYING CALL_NO = 100".
    DISPLAY SQLCODE.
    STOP RUN.
```

UPDATE and DELETE

If an **UPDATE** or **DELETE** is not associated with a **SELECT** that involves a cursor, then the **UPDATE** or **DELETE** does not require a cursor. For example, to remove all computing books from the BOOK table, an application program uses the statement:

> **EXEC SQL DELETE**
> > **FROM** BOOK
> > **WHERE** subject = 'Computing'

Similarly, to change the title for book *300* to *Modula 2* from *Modula-2*, an application program uses:

> EXEC SQL UPDATE BOOK
> > SET title = 'Modula 2'
> > **WHERE** call_no = 300

The **DELETE** and **UPDATE** illustrated here may be incorporated into programs in the same manner as the **SELECT** given in example 8.1.

8.4 Programming with Cursors

In some situations, an application program must access rows individually. To do so, it requires a *cursor*. The cursor is a mechanism to permit the program to process rows one-by-one, and may be thought of as a pointer to the current row. To move the cursor on to the next row, the program uses a **FETCH** statement. Accessing rows individually is similar to the sequential processing of a file.

A program must declare each cursor it uses. The form of the **DECLARE CURSOR** statement is

> **EXEC SQL DECLARE** cursor-name **CURSOR**
> > **FOR** select-expression

For example,

> **EXEC SQL DECLARE** c **CURSOR**
>   **FOR SELECT** title
>   **FROM** BOOK
>   **WHERE** subject = :SUBAREA

defines a cursor for books in a specific subject area. The above statement is declarative; the actual rows are not retrieved until the cursor is **OPEN**ed and rows are **FETCH**ed.

If a cursor is not used with a *positioned* **UPDATE** or **DELETE**(discussed in a later section), then an optional **ORDER BY** clause may be included:

> **EXEC SQL DECLARE** c **CURSOR**
>   **FOR SELECT** title
>   **FROM** BOOK
>   **WHERE** subject = :SUBAREA
>   **ORDER BY** title

Some SQL systems such as DB2 and ORACLE, include another optional clause: the **FOR UPDATE OF** clause. **FOR UPDATE OF** is used to specify fields that are updated in a positioned update and cannot be specified with **ORDER BY.** For example,

> **EXEC SQL DECLARE** q **CURSOR**
>   **FOR SELECT** user_id, fine
>   **FROM** LOAN
>   **WHERE** paid = 'no'
>   **FOR UPDATE OF** fine

Embedded SQL contains **OPEN, FETCH,** and **CLOSE** statements to manage cursors.

OPEN	the rows associated with a cursor are made available
FETCH	the next row of a response set is accessed, and fields from that row are placed into host variables
CLOSE	the cursor is made unavailable (but it can be reopened again)

Example 8.2 Suppose we must retrieve all books in a subject area, but the subject area is not known until the program is running. We use the following cursor.

EXEC SQL DECLARE c **CURSOR FOR**
      SELECT call_no, title
      FROM BOOK
      WHERE subject = :SUBAREA

A **COBOL** program to retrieve the books.

```
IDENTIFICATION DIVISION.
PROGRAM-ID. EX82.

ENVIRONMENT DIVISION.
   CONFIGURATION SECTION.
   DATA DIVISION.

   WORKING-STORAGE SECTION.
      EXEC SQL BEGIN DECLARE SECTION END-EXEC.
   01   SUBAREA PIC X(12) VALUE SPACES.
   01   CALLNO PIC S9999 COMP-5.
   01   TITLE PIC X(30).
      EXEC SQL END DECLARE SECTION END-EXEC.
      EXEC SQL INCLUDE SQLCA END-EXEC.

PROCEDURE DIVISION.
   PERFORM B200-CODE.
   STOP RUN.

B200-CODE.

* EXCEPTION HANDLING
   EXEC SQL WHENEVER NOT FOUND CONTINUE
   END-EXEC.
   EXEC SQL WHENEVER SQLERROR GOTO ERROR-RTN
   END-EXEC.
```

```
* OBTAIN SUBJECT FROM USER
     DISPLAY "ENTER SUBJECT:"
     ACCEPT SUBAREA.

* THE CURSOR FOR THE MULTI-ROW SELECT
     EXEC SQL DECLARE c CURSOR FOR
        SELECT call_no, title
           FROM book WHERE subject = :SUBAREA
     END-EXEC.

* RETRIEVE THE ROWS
     PERFORM OPEN-CURSOR.
     PERFORM GET-ROWS UNTIL SQLCODE NOT EQUAL 0.
     EXEC SQL CLOSE C END-EXEC.

   OPEN-CURSOR.
     EXEC SQL OPEN C END-EXEC.
     EXEC SQL
        FETCH C INTO :CALLNO, :TITLE
     END-EXEC.

   GET-ROWS.
     DISPLAY callno, title.
     EXEC SQL
        FETCH c INTO :CALLNO, :TITLE
     END-EXEC.

   ERROR-RTN.
     DISPLAY "ERROR, SQLCODE=" SQLCODE.
     EXEC SQL CLOSE C END-EXEC.
```

Updating the current record

The SQL statements **UPDATE** and **DELETE** can be used to modify or remove the record currently accessed via a cursor. These versions are referred to as *positioned* **UPDATE** and *positioned* **DELETE**. The syntax for the **UPDATE** is:

> **EXEC SQL UPDATE** TABLE
> **SET** field1 = expression, . . .
> **WHERE CURRENT OF** cursor name

The syntax for the **DELETE** is:

> **EXEC SQL DELETE** TABLE
> **WHERE CURRENT OF** cursor-name

Example 8.3 Suppose the library requires an application that accesses loan rows and which does the following:

a) removes any unpaid fines (deletes the row) for seniors

b) increases any other unpaid fines by 10%.

The programming may be accomplished with a cursor where a **FETCH** is sometimes followed by an **UPDATE** and sometimes by a **DELETE**. We give the cursor first and then the basic logic.

> Cursor:
> > **SELECT** call_no, user_id, fine
> > **FROM** LOAN
> > **WHERE** fine < > 0 **AND** paid = 'no'

> Basic Logic:
> > for each loan record retrieved:
> > > obtain the age for the patron
> > > if the patron's age > = 65, delete the loan row
> > > otherwise increase the fine by 10%

IDENTIFICATION DIVISION.
PROGRAM-ID. EX83.

ENVIRONMENT DIVISION
CONFIGURATION SECTION.
DATA DIVISION.

WORKING-STORAGE SECTION.
*
      EXEC SQL BEGIN DECLARE SECTION END-EXEC.
*
01   CALLNO   PIC S9999 COMP-5.
01   PATID   PIC S9999 COMP-5.
01   FINE   PIC S99999V99 COMP-3.
01   AGE   PIC S9999 COMP-5.

      EXEC SQL END DECLARE SECTION END-EXEC.
      EXEC SQL INCLUDE SQLCA END-EXEC.
*

PROCEDURE DIVISION.

      PERFORM B200-CODE.
      EXEC SQL COMMIT WORK END-EXEC.
      STOP RUN.

B200-CODE.

* EXCEPTION HANDLING
      EXEC SQL
        WHENEVER NOT FOUND CONTINUE
      END-EXEC.
      EXEC SQL
        WHENEVER SQLERROR GOTO ERROR-RTN
      END-EXEC.

* THE CURSOR FOR THE MULTI-ROW SELECT

      EXEC SQL DECLARE c **CURSOR FOR**
      SELECT call_no, user_id, fine
      FROM LOAN
      WHERE fine < > 0 **AND** paid = 'no'
      FOR UPDATE OF fine
      END-EXEC.

```
* GET AND UPDATE THE ROWS
      PERFORM OPEN-CURSOR.
      PERFORM GET-ROWS UNTIL SQLCODE NOT EQUAL 0.
      EXEC SQL CLOSE C END-EXEC.

OPEN-CURSOR.
      EXEC SQL OPEN C END-EXEC.
      IF SQLCODE = 0 THEN
         EXEC SQL
            FETCH C INTO :CALLNO, :PATID, :FINE
         END-EXEC.

GET-ROWS.
   EXEC SQL
      SELECT age INTO :AGE
      FROM PATRON
      WHERE user_id = :PATID
   END-EXEC.

   IF AGE IS NOT LESS THAN 65 THEN
      EXEC SQL DELETE FROM LOAN
         WHERE CURRENT OF C
      END-EXEC
      DISPLAY "LOAN RECORD DELETED FOR ", PATID
   ELSE
      EXEC SQL UPDATE LOAN
            SET FINE = FINE*1.1
            WHERE CURRENT OF C
      END-EXEC
      DISPLAY "LOAN RECORD UPDATED FOR ", PATID.

   EXEC SQL
      FETCH C INTO :CALLNO, :PATID, :FINE
   END-EXEC.

ERROR-RTN.
   DISPLAY "ERROR OCCURRED ", SQLCODE
   EXEC SQL CLOSE C END-EXEC.
```

8.5 DB2 Dynamic SQL

Dynamic SQL permits a programmer to generate a SQL statement at execution time and then pass it on to the database system for execution. It is not necessary to predefine every SQL statement used to the system as is necessary with standard embedded SQL.

One use for such a facility would be to permit one to write a custom interface (perhaps not at all like SQL) for a set of users to allow access to the SQL system without having to learn SQL itself. The program would interpret the user's request according to certain rules, generate the equivalent SQL, pass that on for execution, and then return the results to the user.

We discuss **SELECT** first, followed by a discussion of other statements.

SELECT

To use the **SELECT** statement dynamically involves:

- a cursor
- a variable to hold the statement
- *preparing* the statement for execution
- obtaining a *description* of the result of the select
- opening the cursor
- fetching rows of the response
- closing the cursor

Two new steps introduced are *preparing* and *describing* a **SELECT.** The **PREPARE** step causes the database system to analyze the **SELECT** and prepare an execution plan for it. With static embedded SQL, this process was performed by a precompiler. The **DESCRIBE** step provides the application program with information about the columns in the result. In very general cases, the application program doesn't know (at the time of coding) the contents of the results. This step is required to obtain information about the fields and their data types in a row of the response.

Once **DESCRIBE** has been used, the application program can allocate the needed variables for the result. The specifications for **DESCRIBE** are complex enough that it is best to refer the interested reader to IBM manuals on this matter. **DESCRIBE** is only permitted when coding in PL/I since it is the only language which provides the execution-time allocation of variables that is required here. Note that **DESCRIBE** is needed only when the programmer does not know the format of the result at coding time.

Other Statements

To execute other statement types one uses the following **EXEC SQL** statements:

- **DECLARE** specifies the name of the SQL variable which will hold the statement.
- **PREPARE** has the database system analyze the command and prepare a plan for its execution.
- **EXECUTE** has the request executed.

For example, to update a book (call number provided at execution time) by changing its title (new title provided at execution time) can be accomplished by the following:

```
EXEC SQL BEGIN DECLARE SECTION;
DCL PLISTMT CHAR(256) VARYING;
DCL TITLE CHAR(256) VARYING;
DCL CALLNO CHAR(256) VARYING;
EXEC SQL END DECLARE SECTION;
EXEC SQL DECLARE SQLSTMT;

GET LIST (CALLNO);
GET LIST (TITLE);
PLISTMT = 'UPDATE BOOK SET TITLE = ' || title ||
        'WHERE CALLNO = ' || callno;
EXEC SQL PREPARE SQLSTMT FROM :PLISTMT;
EXEC SQL EXECUTE SQLSTMT;
IF SQLCODE ^= 0 THEN .....
```

DB2 permits programs to PREPARE the following statements for execution:

ALTER, COMMENT, COMMIT, CREATE, DELETE, DROP, EXPLAIN, GRANT, INSERT, SELECT (without **INTO** clause), **REVOKE, ROLLBACK**

DB2 does not permit references to host variables, but a similar effect can be obtained through the use of parameters in the EXEC SQL EXECUTE statement. Interested readers should consult the IBM manuals for further details.

8.6 PL/I Examples

We have included PL/I versions of the COBOL programs presented earlier. Each program has been tested, and has run correctly on an SQL system.

Example 8.4   A PL/I program to retrieve book 100:

```
EX 84: PROCEDURE OPTIONS (MAIN);

/* DECLARATIONS */
EXEC SQL INCLUDE SQLCA;
EXEC SQL BEGIN DECLARE SECTION ;
DCL SUBAREA      CHARACTER (12);
DCL SINDIC       FIXED BIN (15);
DCL TITLE        CHARACTER (30);
EXEC SQL END DECLARE SECTION ;

/* EXCEPTION HANDLING */
EXEC SQL WHENEVER NOT FOUND CONTINUE;
EXEC SQL WHENEVER SQLERROR CONTINUE;

/* RETRIEVE THE TITLE FOR 100 */
EXEC SQL SELECT subject, title
     INTO :SUBAREA:SINDIC, :TITLE
```

```
        FROM BOOK WHERE call number = 100;

/* CHECK STATUS OF SQL STATEMENT */
IF SQLCODE = 0 THEN
        IF SINDIC = -1 THEN
            PUT SKIP LIST (TITLE, '***NULL***');
        ELSE PUT SKIP LIST (TITLE,SUBAREA)
ELSE DO;
        PUT SKIP LIST ('ERROR OCCURRED');
        PUT SKIP LIST (SQLCODE=',SQLCODE);
END;
END EX84;
```

Example 8.5   A PL/I program to retrieve and display the books:

```
EX85: PROCEDURE OPTIONS (MAIN);

/* DECLARATIONS */
EXEC SQL INCLUDE SQLCA;
EXEC SQL BEGIN DECLARE SECTION;
DCL SUBAREA        CHARACTER (12);
DCL TITLE          CHARACTER (30);
DCL CALLNO         FIXED BIN (15);
EXEC SQL END DECLARE SECTION ;

/* EXCEPTION HANDLING */
EXEC SQL WHENEVER NOT FOUND CONTINUE;
EXEC SQL WHENEVER SQLERROR GOTO DBERROR;

/* THE CURSOR */
EXEC SQL DECLARE c CURSOR FOR
        SELECT call_no, title
        FROM BOOK
        WHERE subject = :SUBAREA

/* GET THE SUBJECT AREA */
GET LIST (SUBAREA);

/* OPEN THE CURSOR */
EXEC SQL OPEN c;
```

```
/* RETRIEVE THE ROWS ONE-BY-ONE */
EXEC SQL FETCH c INTO :CALLNO, :TITLE;
DO WHILE (SQLCODE=0);
        PUT SKIP LIST (callno, title);
        EXEC SQL FETCH c INTO :CALLNO, :TITLE;
END;
EXEC SQL CLOSE c;
RETURN;

/* PROGRAM ERROR HANDLING CODE */
DBERROR:
        PUT SKIP LIST (SQLCODE);
        EXEC SQL ROLLBACK;
        RETURN;
END EX85;
```

Example 8.6 Update the LOAN table: remove unpaid entries for seniors and increase other unpaid fines by 10%

```
EX86: PROCEDURE OPTIONS (MAIN);

/* DECLARATIONS */

EXEC SQL INCLUDE SQLCA;
EXEC SQL BEGIN DECLARE SECTION ;
DCL CALL NO      FIXED BIN (15);
DCL PATID        FIXED BIN(15);
DCL FINE         FIXED DEC(8,2);
DCL AGE          FIXED BIN(15);
DCL DBERROR CONDITION;
EXEC SQL END DECLARE SECTION ;

/* EXCEPTION HANDLING */
EXEC SQL WHENEVER NOT FOUND CONTINUE;
EXEC SQL WHENEVER SQLERROR CONTINUE;

ON CONDITION (DBERROR)
BEGIN;
PUT SKIP LIST ( 'BAD ERROR, SQLCODE = ',SQLCODE);
```

```
EXEC SQL ROLLBACK;
GO TO STOPPGM;
END;

/* THE CURSOR */

EXEC SQL DECLARE c CURSOR FOR
    SELECT call_no, user_id, fine
    FROM LOAN
    WHERE fine < > 0 AND paid = 'no'
    FOR UPDATE OF fine;

/* OPEN THE CURSOR */

EXEC SQL OPEN c;
IF SQLCODE ^ = 0 THEN
        SIGNAL CONDITION (DBERROR);

/* RETRIEVE THE ROWS ONE-BY-ONE */

/* INITIAL FETCH */
EXEC SQL FETCH c INTO :CALLNO, :PATID, :FINE;
IF (SQLCODE ^ = 0 & SQLCODE ^ = 100)
    THEN SIGNAL CONDITION (DBERROR);

DO WHILE (SQLCODE = 0);
    /* SINGLETON SELECT TO GET USER'S AGE */
    EXEC SQL    SELECT age INTO :AGE FROM PATRON
            WHERE user_id = :PATID;
    IF AGE > = 65 THEN
    EXEC SQL            DELETE FROM LOAN
                    WHERE CURRENT OF c;
    EXEC SQL FETCH c into
        :CALLNO, :PATID, :FINE;
    IF (SQLCODE ^ = 0 & SQLCODE ^ = 100)
            THEN SIGNAL CONDITION (DBERROR);
    END;
EXEC SQL CLOSE C;
STOPPGM:
END EX86;
```

Exercises

8.1 What is the structure of SQL statements embedded within a host language? What is the function of the **DECLARE SECTION** statement?

8.2 Write a complete program in COBOL illustrating retrieval of a customer record from the CUSTOMER table.

8.3 Insert new transactions into the TRANSACTIONS table. Write a program to prepare monthly bank statements for the above customers of International Bank. It should list all the transactions that occurred during the month, the beginning balance, and the closing (ending) balance for the period.

8.4. Write a program to

a) add a customer to the CUSTOMER table

b) delete a customer from the CUSTOMER table

8.5 Write a program to change the customer rating in the CUSTOMER table. Assume that the information is provided interactively.

Part

SQL Database Systems

9
ORACLE

Oracle Corporation's ORACLE is a popular relational database management system that supports SQL. The user interface and SQL language are compatible with both IBM's DB2 and SQL/DS. ORACLE comes with a complete set of support tools, such as an application generator, a report writer, a forms generator, and an Integrated Data Dictionary. ORACLE is designed for a multi-user environment. Their current release adds transaction processing to the ORACLE-distributed DBMS.

In this chapter we continue to illustrate SQL with examples but in the context of ORACLE. The information presented in this chapter will *walk* you through a complete SQL session using our library database as a model. You will have an opportunity to create tables, insert or load data, and update tables.

9.1 ORACLE Environment

The ORACLE environment consists of the following components: a relational database management system, an active data dictionary, SQL query language, application generator, and report writer. A brief description of ORACLE's family of application development tools is presented below:

SQL*PLUS   Provides direct interface to the ORACLE relational database system. Contains the full implementation of ANSI SQL.

SQL*FORMS   Provides a user-friendly interface to query, update, and add information.

SQL*REPORT   Generates reports.

SQL* MENU   Creates a menu-driven system by integrating different functions.

SQL* GRAPH   Generates a graphic description of data.

EASY* SQL   Provides a friendly SQL interface for the end user.

SQL* QMX   Provides a Query-By-Example interface. Comparable to IBM's Query Management Facility (QMF).

DICTIONARY   Helps manage the application development process — part of the CASE family

SQL* STAR   A distributed DBMS that supports ORACLE, DB2, and SQL/DS on multiple, dissimilar host computers.

ORACLE/Net   A distributed database access to remote computers using ORACLE.

ORACLE/Link   Transfers data between microcomputers and mainframes using ORACLE.

Unlike SQL/DS and DB2 which run only on IBM mainframes, ORACLE runs on IBM mainframes, DEC, and several other manufacturers' computing environments. There is considerable portability, as all versions of ORACLE are identical and include the full implementation of SQL. In addition, ORACLE's network software allows networking of microcomputers, minicomputers, and mainframes, and permits sharing of databases. (See also table 9.1 for ORACLE specifications).

Table 9.1   ORACLE Specifications

Tables in a database	no limit
Rows in a table	no limit
Columns in a table	254
Characters in a field	240
Characters in a row	126,495
Digits in a number field	105
Indexes on a table	no limit
Tables or views joined in a query	no limit
Levels of nested subqueries	255

9.2 SQL*PLUS

SQL*PLUS provides a direct interface to ORACLE and contains a full implementation of SQL. We use SQL*PLUS to:

- create tables
- store and retrieve information from tables
- modify information in the tables
- manage the database
- assist with data sharing and providing a security

The various SQL examples described in Part A can be readily executed using ORACLE's SQL, therefore, only SQL extensions, and important SQL*PLUS commands are presented in this chapter.

EASY*SQL provides an alternative to using SQL*PLUS. It consists of menus and panels and is easier to learn and use, though limited in its capability. For instance, only three tables can be joined, and we cannot **GRANT** access to any user. Another Oracle product SQL*QMX also provides a user-friendly interface to solve queries — it uses a Query-By-Example approach.

9.3 Using SQL*PLUS

A *username* and *password* is needed in order to run SQL*PLUS. This is normally generated by the database administrator or system manager. On a single-user system, this task may be performed by the user.

Start up

The following steps will enable you to enter SQL*PLUS:

1. Turn on the computer; you are now at the operating system prompt.

2. Microcomputer users only, type **ORACLE** to run the DBMS.

3. Type **SQLPLUS** at the operating system prompt.

4. At the prompt, *"Enter user-name:"*, enter your **username**

5. At the prompt, *"Enter password:"*, enter your **password**

6. You are now in SQL*PLUS, and will see the SQL*PLUS prompt "SQL >"

Leaving SQL*PLUS

In order to quit the SQL*PLUS session type the command, **EXIT**:

SQL >   **EXIT**

Since ORACLE is resident in the memory, you may want to stop it and remove it completely. This can be done by typing **IOR SHUT** followed by **REMORA ALL**.

Note that you do not have to exit SQL*PLUS in order to access the operating system. This is done by typing **HOST** followed by any legal operating system command. For example:

SQL >   **HOST DIR*.***

Typing **HOST** by itself will let you work at the operating system prompt as long as you need to, until **EXIT** is typed again. This returns you to SQL*PLUS again.

9.3.1 The command line

At the "SQL>" prompt you can enter two types of commands: SQL Commands and SQL*PLUS Commands. Both are described next:

SQL commands

An SQL command is used in an ORACLE database to create, retrieve, and modify information. It is stored in the SQL buffer and it remains there until a new command is entered. The example below employs the SQL command **SELECT** additional SQL commands available in ORACLE include **ALTER, AUDIT, CREATE, DELETE, DROP, GRANT, INSERT, LOCK, RENAME, ROLLBACK,** and **UPDATE.** All SQL statements must end with a semicolon.

        SQL >   **SELECT** *
          2   **FROM** LOAN;

If a return is pressed, the editor automatically takes you to the next line, which it numbers (line 2 in this case). Thus, long queries can meaningfully be broken down into several lines.

SQL*PLUS commands

SQL*PLUS Commands are used to format output, create reports, and edit SQL commands. Unlike the commands discussed above, SQL*PLUS commands are not stored in the SQL buffer. Some examples of SQL*PLUS commands are: **BTITLE, COLUMN, EXIT, SHOW, SPOOL,** and **START.** Also, all commands presented in TABLE 9.2 are examples of SQL*PLUS commands.

The following SQL*PLUS command can be used to format the output of the query described above:

SQL>   **COLUMN** fine **FORMAT** $9,999.99 **HEADING** Fines

Type **RUN** to execute the query. If required, SQL*PLUS commands can be continued on to the next line by using a hyphen, see example below.

        COLUMN fine **FORMAT** $9,999.99 –
        HEADING Fines

9.3.2 Editing and correcting mistakes

The editing commands described in Table 9.2 can be used to change the contents of the SQL*PLUS buffer. Commands other than **LIST** or **RUN,** affect only a single line. This line is identified by the asterisk placed after the line number.

Table 9.2 SQL Editing Commands

Abbreviation	Purpose
A Text	Append text at the end of a line
C/old/new/	Change old text to new
C/old/	Change old (removes it)
CL BUFF	CLears all text in BUFFer
DEL	DELete a line
I	Input lines into existing text
L	List all lines in the buffer
L n	List nth line
L m n	List a range of lines, m to n
RUN	RUN the current SQL command

To make several changes, you might want to use a word processor or an editor. The host system's editor can be activated from SQL*PLUS by typing:

SQL >   **EDIT**

The editor EDLIN is activated for MS-DOS—based microcomputers. You can now edit the contents of the current buffer. The changes are saved automatically in the buffer of SQL*PLUS when you exit the editor or word processor.

9.3.3 Storing and printing query results

It is often convenient to store the results of a session in a file for editing or printing in a word processor. The **SPOOL** command can be used for that purpose. At the start of a session, one designates a spool filename:

SQL >   **SPOOL** filename

On completion of a query session, you may want to print the file right away. To print the file enter the command:

SQL >   **SPOOL OUT**

Note that in a single-user system, the spool might not be released until you quit SQL*PLUS or type HOST.

Alternatively, if you are interested in editing the above file in a word processor, type:

SQL >   **SPOOL OFF**

This will create a *list* file with an *LST* extension. You can now print the file directly from your word processor.

Saving queries in a command file

It is possible to save SQL and SQL*PLUS commands for later use. We have two options here:

- Save and retrieve SQL commands, but not SQL*PLUS commands
- Save and retrieve both SQL and SQL*PLUS commands

Save and retrieve SQL commands

In order to save a SQL query, we simply type **SAVE,** followed by the file name. Note that you have to use a unique file name each time you save; otherwise, ORACLE will simply replace the contents of the old file with the new. It does not give you a warning.

SQL >   **SAVE** file_name

To retrieve the file enter:

> SQL>   **GET** file_name

This will retrieve the contents of the file and display it on the screen. You can edit the command now, or execute it with the **RUN** command.

Save and retrieve both SQL & SQL*PLUS commands

To save and retrieve SQL*PLUS commands, such as "**COLUMN** fine **FORMAT** $999.99" and "SET AUTOCOMMIT ON"; you may want to use the host system's editor. With it you can create batch reports or command files containing both SQL and SQL*PLUS commands. Consider the example below:

> SQL>   **EDIT** *filename*
> 1   column title heading 'Book Title'
> 2   **SELECT**
> 3   **FROM** BOOK;

Note: It is important that you terminate only SQL (not SQL*PLUS) commands using a semicolon. Save the file and exit the system editor.

You can execute this file using the **START** command.

> SQL>   **START** *filename*

9.3.4 Getting *Help*

The procedure for obtaining help while in SQL*PLUS is simply to type the command **HELP**, followed by the subject on which you need help. Consider the example below:

> **HELP** insert

You can also obtain a list of all SQL and SQL*PLUS commands by typing:

HELP topics

9.4   Creating a Table

To create a table using ORACLE, the **CREATE TABLE** command is used as described in chapter 2. The tables of the library database are displayed again in figure 9.1. The following data types are used in the DDL examples below: **NUMBER, CHAR, DATE** and **INTEGER**. In ORACLE the **DATE** data type has the following default format: DD-MMM-YY. i.e., 05-AUG-88. Also, while **NUMBER** can be used to define both real numbers and whole numbers, **INTEGER** is used to define whole numbers only.

We specify the columns and data type for each field of the table. The completed DDL used to create the BOOK table appears below:

```
CREATE TABLE BOOK (
        call_no      NUMBER(3) NOT NULL
        title        CHAR(30)NOT NULL
        subject      CHAR(12));
```

The LOAN table and the PATRON table can be created similarly.

```
CREATE TABLE LOAN (
        call_no      NUMBER(3)          NOT NULL
        user_id      NUMBER(3)          NOT NULL
        date_due     DATE               NOT NULL
        date_ret     DATE,
        fine         NUMBER(7,2),
        paid         CHAR(3));

CREATE TABLE PATRON (
        user_id      NUMBER             NOT NULL
        name         CHAR(15)           NOT NULL
```

Figure 9.1 Contents of tables in the Library database

BOOK

call_no	title	subject
100	Physics Handbook	Physics
200	Database Systems	Computing
300	Modula-2	Computing
400	Database Design	Computing
500	Software Testing	Computing
600	Business Society	Business
700	Graphs	Mathematics
800	Cell Biology	Biology
900	Set Theory	Mathematics

LOAN

call_no	user_id	date_due	date_ret	fine	paid
100	100	12-SEP-88	01-SEP-88		
300	100	01-SEP-88			
900	200	01-SEP-88	20-DEC-88	1.90	yes
400	200	04-DEC-89	16-MAY-90	16.30	yes
600	200	04-DEC-89	16-MAY-90	16.30	yes
500	250	02-OCT-84			
600	250	02-OCT-84	02-OCT-85	36.50	yes
700	300	10-DEC-88	01-DEC-88		
800	350	01-DEC-88	30-DEC-88	2.90	yes
900	400	01-OCT-90			

PATRON

user_id	name	age
100	Wong	22
150	Colin	31
200	King	21
250	Das	67
300	Niall	17
350	Smith	72
400	Jones	41

An SQL*PLUS command called **DESCRIBE** can be used to display the columns and data types.

SQL >   **DESCRIBE** BOOK

Result:	Name	Null?	Type
	call_no	not null	number(3)
	title	not null	char(30)
	subject		char(12)

Displaying the structure of the table this way is quite useful, especially when we forget a column name or data type. **DESCRIBE** is not an ANSI SQL command.

9.5 Inserting Data

Now that we have created the BOOK table, the next logical step is to add records to the tables. With ORACLE we have several options.

9.5.1 INSERT command

The most simple, but cumbersome, option is to use the **INSERT** command.

Example: Insert the following record into the BOOK table:
100, Physics Handbook, Physics

    INSERT INTO BOOK
    VALUES (100, 'Physics Handbook', 'Physics');

The above **INSERT** command has to be used repeatedly to add more rows (i.e., more books) to the database. To facilitate such data entry, ORACLE permits use of parameters that represent values provided when the command is executed. Consider the **INSERT** example below:

INSERT INTO BOOK
VALUES (&call_no, '&title', '&subject');

The parameter & is followed by the name of the column. Since we have put quotes around &*title* and &*subject* we do not need to put quotes around *title* or *subject* when we enter data. (Only **CHAR** or **DATE** values need such quotes around column names, **NUMBER** values do not.) On executing the above **INSERT** statement, ORACLE provides us the following prompts:

Enter value for call_no.
Enter value for title:
Enter value for subject:

If the following values are entered:

Enter value for call_no: 850
Enter value for title: Database Machines
Enter value for subject: Computing

the outcome is (insert statement generated automatically):

INSERT INTO BOOK
VALUES (850, 'Database Machines', 'Computing');

ORACLE will default to **NULL** if a column is not included in the **INSERT** statement. Also, we can specify NULL in the corresponding **VALUES** clause to insert **NULL** values:

INSERT INTO BOOK
VALUES (850, 'Database Machines', **NULL**);

To enter a date, quotes must be put around the values: '07-DEC-87'. Unless parameters are used we can automatically enter today's date by using **SYSDATE** as follows:

INSERT INTO LOAN
VALUES (900, 850, '10-Feb-90', **SYSDATE, NULL, NULL**);

Here the date that a book is returned (*date_ret*) is inserted automatically.

9.5.2   Using SQL*LOADER

ORACLE's SQL*LOADER utility program allows you to import data from non-ORACLE files into ORACLE tables. It is similar to IBM's DB2 LOAD utility and is very flexible. It can load data from multiple source data files of different types. It can load fixed-format, delimited-format and variable-length records. It also provides useful status reports of the load process.

The diagram below illustrates the process. The input files to and output files from SQL*LOADER are illustrated.

Input
        Control Information ──────────> SQL*LOADER
        plus
        Data to be loaded

Output
                                        Bad File
        SQL*LOADER ──────────────> Discard File
                                        Log File

In order to load data using SQL*LOADER, it must be provided not only with data but also control information. The control information describes the data, the format, the location of data and target files, and the specifications for loading data.

The Log File contains table, data-file, and other global information. The Bad File is always created and consists of rejected records. The Discard File describes records that do not meet control file specifications; it is only created if specified in the **LOAD DATA** command (see below). The loading process is illustrated:

Example: Populate the BOOK table with the records
                described in figure 9.1

A two-step process is required to achieve this:

a) Create a file called **BOOK.CTL** with the following:

LOAD DATA
INFILE *
APPEND
INTO TABLE BOOK
FIELDS TERMINATED BY " , " **OPTIONALLY ENCLOSED BY** ' " '
(call_no,title,subject)
BEGINDATA
100,"Physics Handbook","Physics"
200,"Database Systems","Computing"
300,"Modula-2","Computing"
400,"Database Design","Computing"
500,"Software Testing","Computing"
600,"Business Society","Business"
700,"Graphs","Mathematics"
800,"Cell Biology","Biology"
900,"Set Theory","Mathematics"

b) Invoke the SQL*LOADER by typing the following command:

SQLLOAD USERID = username/password, **CONTROL** = BOOK.CTL

On execution of the above command, you will get a final message indicating the number of books committed to the database. In order to determine the real status of the **LOAD** operation, it is important to look into the two output files produced by the utility—the Log File and the Bad File. The Log File shows the structure of the input data and the Bad File describes the rejected records. In the above example, **INFILE** * indicates that data is included within the control file. If the data file is located elsewhere, the filename is specified instead.

Example: Describe a control file to populate the LOAN table (records are described in figure 9.1).

The following information needs to be provided in a control file:

LOAD DATA
INFILE *
APPEND
INTO TABLE LOAN
FIELDS TERMINATED BY " , " **OPTIONALLY ENCLOSED BY** ' " '
(call_no, user_id, date_due *DATE* "yyyy-mm-dd",
date_ret *DATE* "yyyy-mm-dd", fine)
BEGINDATA
100,100,19880901,19880912,
300,100,19880901,
900,200,19880901,19880920,1.90
400,200,19871205,19880516,16.30
600,200,19871205,19880516,16.30
500,250,19841002,
600,250,19841002,19851002,36.50
700,300,19881201,19881210,
800,350,19881201,19881230,2.90
900,400,19871001,

9.5.3 Using SQL*FORMS

We can also use the SQL*FORMS utility to enter data into the BOOK table. It is useful to design a form if on-line data entry is done; also SQL*FORMS support data integrity by placing constraints on the data being entered. A very simple example is provided here to illustrate the use of SQL*FORMS. For more information, consult ORACLE's SQL*FORMS manual. Let us create a default form for entering new books into the book table. Press the [F10] function key to accept.

The first step is to log-on by typing:

SQLFORMS username/PASSWORD

A menu appears on the screen. To start, type **BOOKFORM** under "Name." Tab to **CREATE** and press [F2] (the select key). You will now see a "CHOOSE BLOCK" menu. Type **BOOK**. Next Tab to "DEFAULT." A default block menu will appear. Change "Rows Displayed" from **1** to **9**. Press **[F10]** twice to indicate completion. Then at the main menu, select "Generate." Press **[F10]**. A message appears indicating that a form has been generated. Press **[F10]** once again and select "SAVE" by pressing **[F2]**. The form is now ready for use. To use BOOKFORM at the operating system prompt type:

RUNFORM BOOKFORM username/password

Enter new books and when asked if you want to commit the data, type **Y**.

9.6 Querying Tables

Since ORACLE SQL is compatible with ANSI SQL, the various examples presented in PART A of this book can now be tried out using ORACLE.

As indicated earlier, SQL*PLUS provides several additional functions and commands to improve the display of the results. The next section introduces the various commands that assist us with the task.

9.6.1 Working with number values

In order to display numbers using formats we can use the following SQL*PLUS template:

"**COLUMN** *column-name* **FORMAT** *picture*,"

Example: Display all *user_id*'s that have to pay a fine.

SQL>   **COLUMN** fines **FORMAT** $99.99

SQL>   **SELECT** user_id, fine

2   **FROM** LOAN

3   **WHERE** fine **IS NOT NULL**;

Result:	**user_id**	**fine**
	200	$ 1.90
	200	$16.30
	200	$16.30
	250	$36.50
	350	$ 2.90

Other useful Format Pictures are described below:

Format	**Value**	**Will Display As**
9,999.99	1118.469	1,118.47
0999	25	0025
B999	0	(Blanks displayed for 0)
999.99	2000.50	###.## (value too large)
'Mon dd, yyyy'	02101990	Feb 10, 1990

9.6.2   Using column header aliases

The column heading that is displayed is generally the one that was specified when the table was created. Sometimes it is desirable to have a different heading display as it describes the column heading more clearly. With SQL*PLUS we can do so by specifying an *alias header* in the select clause.

   Example: SELECT user_id, name "Patron Name", age
   FROM PATRON

Result:	**user_id**	**Patron Name**	**age**
	100	Wong	22
	150	Colin	31
	200	King	21
	250	Das	67
	300	Niall	17
	350	Smith	72
	400	Jones	41

If an alias contains special characters such as a space, slash (/), or asterisk (*) it must be enclosed in double quotes, as illustrated above; otherwise quotes are not required.

9.6.3 Formatting a query into a report

Most database systems, including ORACLE, provide us with report generators that enable us to create and modify reports easily. However, it might be useful occasionally to create quick-and-dirty reports without such tools. With ORACLE we can enhance the output of SQL queries by using statements such as **TTITLE, BTITLE, COMPUTE, BREAK** and **COLUMN**.

Example: Generate a report describing the collection of fines.

```
COLUMN title HEADING 'Book title'
COLUMN fine HEADING 'User Fines' FORMAT $999.99
BREAK ON title SKIP 1
COMPUTE SUM OF fine ON title
TTITLE 'COLLECTION OF FINES'
BTITLE '– confidential–'
        SELECT title, fine
        FROM BOOK, LOAN
        WHERE book.call_no = loan.call_no
        AND fine IS NOT NULL
        ORDER BY title;
```

Here we rename the default column header *title* to *Book Title*, and the header *fine* to *User Fines*. The **BREAK** command creates a control break by title; **COMPUTE SUM** adds fines by title; **TTITLE** creates the top title (date and page number are inserted automatically at the top of each page); **BTITLE** creates the bottom title. All SQL*PLUS commands remain enabled until you either reset them, quit the session, or disable them with commands, such as **TTITLE OFF, BTITLE OFF, COLUMN TITLE CLEAR, CLEAR COMPUTE,** and **CLEAR BREAK.**

Fri Dec 25   COLLECTION OF FINES   Page 1

Book Title	User Fines
Business Society	$16.30
	$36.50
* * * * * * * * * *	
sum	$52.80
Cell Biology	$2.90
* * * * * * * * * *	
sum	$2.90
Database Design	$16.30
* * * * * * * * * *	
sum	$16.30
Set Theory	$1.90
* * * * * * * * * *	
sum	$1.90

–confidential–

9.7 ORACLE System Catalog

The system catalog consists of a group of tables that contain information about tables, views, user access privileges and other features of the ORACLE DBMS.

A list of all ORACLE tables that make up the ORACLE catalog can be obtained as follows.

```
SQL >    SELECT *
  2      FROM dtab;
```

Result: See table 9.3

Table 9.3 ORACLE Tables

TNAME	Remarks
AUDIT_ACCESS	Audits entries for accesses to user's tables/views (DBA sees all)
AUDIT_ACTIONS	Maps auditing action numbers to action names
AUDIT_CONNECT	Audits trail entries for user log-on/log-off (DBA sees all users)
AUDIT_DBA	Audits trail entries for DBA activities — for DBA use only
AUDIT_EXISTS	Audits trail entries for objects which do NOT EXIST— DBA use only
AUDIT_TRAIL	Audits trail entries relevant to the user (DBA sees all)
CATALOG	Tables and views accessible to user (excluding data dictionary)
CLUSTERS	Clusters and their tables (accessible to user)
CLUSTERCOLUMNS	Maps cluster columns to clustered table columns
COL	Specifications of columns in tables created by the user
COLUMNS	Columns in tables accessible to user (excluding data dictionary)
DEFAULT_AUDIT	Default table auditing options
DTAB	Description of tables and views in Oracle Data Dictionary
EXTENTS	Data structure of extents within tables
INDEXES	Indexes created by user and indexes on tables created by user
PARTITIONS	File structure of files within partitions— for DBA use only

PRIVATESYN	Private synonyms created by the user
PUBLICSYN	Public synonyms
SESSIONS	Audits trail entries for the user's sessions (DBA sees all)
SPACES	Selection of space definitions for creating tables and clusters
STORAGE	Data and Index storage allocation for user's own tables
SYNONYMS	Synonyms, private and public
SYSAUDIT_TRAIL	Synonym for sys.audit_trail—for DBA use only
SYSCATALOG	Profile of tables and views accessible to the user
SYSCOLAUTH	Directory of column update access granted by or to the user
SYSCOLUMNS	Specifications of columns in accessible tables and views
SYSEXTENTS	Data structure of tables throughout system — for DBA use only
SYSINDEXES	List of indexes, underlying columns, creator, and options
SYSPROGS	List of programs precompiled by user
SYSSTORAGE	Summary of all database storage — for DBA use only
SYSTABALLOC	Data and index space allocations for all tables — for DBA use only
SYSTABAUTH	Director of access authorization granted by or to the user
SYSTEM_AUDIT	System auditing options — for DBA use only
SYSUSERAUTH	Master list of ORACLE users — for DBA use only
SYSUSERLIST	List of ORACLE users
SYSVIEWS	List of accessible views

TAB	List of tables, views, clusters, and synonyms created by the user
TABALLOC	Data and index space allocations for all user's tables
TABQUOTAS	Table allocation (space) parameters for tables created by user
TABLE_AUDIT	Auditing options of user's tables and views (DBA sees all)
VIEWS	Defining SQL statements for views created by the user
DBLINKS	Public and private links to external databases
SYSDBLINKS	All links to external databases — for DBA use only

Further references can be made to any of the tables defined in table 9.3. Let us obtain more information on TAB:

SQL>   **SELECT ***

2   **FROM** TAB;

Result:	TNAME	TABTYPE	CLUSTERID
	BOOK	TABLE	
	FINES	VIEW	
	LOAN	TABLE	
	PATRON	TABLE	

Similarly a list of all tables and views that you have access to can be obtained by querying the CATALOG table and a list of all column definitions can be obtained by querying the COL table.

9.8 CLUSTERing

To improve performance, ORACLE allows us to physically organize the database by *clustering* related data. We can create single- or multiple-column clusters, and we can cluster the rows of one table or several tables. A cluster stores data together on the same physical disk page, making disk access quicker when an equijoin (column values compared for equality) is executed. Clustering saves disk space (as the common column is stored only once) and can improve the performance of SQL operations such as **JOIN, DELETE**, and **UPDATE.**

Creating a one-column cluster

The single-column cluster definition is useful when the same values repeat several times in a particular column. For example in the BOOK table only five *subject* values occur several times. We have to follow two steps to create the single-column cluster:

- Create the cluster on the common column, and
- Load the cluster.

To create this single-column cluster, we type the following command:

SQL >   **CREATE CLUSTER** cl_subject (subject **CHAR**(12));

The BOOK table can now be loaded into the *cl_subject* cluster.

SQL >   **CREATE TABLE** NEW_BOOK_TABLE
2   **CLUSTER** cl_subject(subject)
3   **AS SELECT * FROM** BOOK;

Creating a multiple-column cluster

Multiple-column clusters can be created in the same manner as discussed above. The syntax is similar to the single-column cluster — we simply add additional column names for clusters within the parentheses.

Creating a multiple-table cluster

To illustrate multiple-table clustering, let us consider the library database again. Suppose we are interested in physically clustering the tables BOOK and LOAN on their common column *call_no*. Once again, we have to follow two steps:

* Create the cluster on the common column, and
* Load the cluster.

To create the cluster we type the following command:

SQL >   **CREATE CLUSTER** cl_book (call_no **NUMBER**(3));

We now have a cluster *cl_book* created on *call_no*. The next step is to load the cluster. In order to accomplish this a NEW_BOOK_TABLE is created. In the statements below we create the table and load it into the cluster *cl_user_id.*

SQL >   **CREATE TABLE** NEW_BOOK TABLE
2   **CLUSTER** cl_book (call_no)
3   **AS SELECT** * **FROM** BOOK;

The same is done for the **NEW_LOAN_TABLE.**

SQL >   **CREATE TABLE** NEW_LOAN_TABLE
2   **CLUSTER** cl_book (call_no)
3   **AS SELECT** * **FROM** LOAN;

The tables are now joined together on the same disk page to provide us a faster join. The old BOOK and LOAN tables have to be deleted (dropped).

9.9 Embedded SQL Using ORACLE

It is possible to access the ORACLE database using applications programs. In order to do so, one of ORACLE's interfaces must be used to precompile the Embedded SQL statements into the procedural language. At present, high-level languages such as FORTRAN, Pascal, C, PL/I, and COBOL are supported.

A second interface, called the ORACLE CALL Interface (OCI), also allows high-level language applications to access ORACLE's data. Direct calls to ORACLE subroutines contained in the run-time libraries can be made. With OCI, ORACLE can interface with several high-level languages. Examples of calls available are **CALL OLON**—connect to ORACLE, and **CALL OSOL3**—pass a SQL statement to ORACLE.

Chapter 8 provides detailed description and several examples of SQL commands embedded in an application program using both COBOL and PL/I. However, a simple COBOL example is also provided below to illustrate some important aspects of Embedded SQL peculiar to ORACLE.

Preparing an application for execution

The procedure to prepare an application for execution using Embedded SQL is illustrated below:

1. Source program PROG1 is written (in COBOL for example).
2. PROG1 is precompiled. (Here ORACLE's Pro*COBOL will translate all Embedded SQL statements into source program statements.)
3. PROG1 is compiled, and an object file is created using a commercial compiler compatible with Pro*COBOL.
4. Link-edit the object file — an executable program is now created and can be run.

Sample Pro*COBOL program

A sample COBOL program from chapter 8 is reproduced here to highlight log-in and log-out.

Example: Retrieve *call_no* 100 from the BOOK table.

```
IDENTIFICATION DIVISION.
PROGRAM-ID. EX81.

ENVIRONMENT DIVISION.
CONFIGURATION SECTION.
DATA DIVISION.

WORKING-STORAGE SECTION.

    EXEC SQL BEGIN DECLARE SECTION END-EXEC.

01      SUBAREA     PIC X(12).
01      SINDIC      PIC S9999 COMP-5.
01      TITLE       PIC X(30).
01      USERID      PIC X(7) VALUE SPACES.
01      PASSWRD     PIC X(7) VALUE SPACES.

    EXEC SQL END DECLARE SECTION END-EXEC.
    EXEC SQL INCLUDE SQLCA END-EXEC.

PROCEDURE DIVISION.

A000-LOG-ON.
    PERFORM B100-LOG
    STOP RUN.

B100-LOG.
    DISPLAY "USERNAME?".
    ACCEPT USERID FROM CONSOLE.
    DISPLAY "PASSWORD? ".
    ACCEPT PASSWRD FROM CONSOLE.

    EXEC SQL
    WHENEVER SQLERROR GOTO Z100-LOG-ERROR
    END-EXEC.
```

```
EXEC SQL
CONNECT :USERID IDENTIFIED BY :PASSWORD
END-EXEC.

EXEC SQL
WHENEVER SQLERROR GOTO Z200-LOG-ERROR
END-EXEC.

DISPLAY "CONNECTED TO BOOK DATABASE . . . " .
MOVE SPACES TO TITLE, SUBAREA.

EXEC SQL
    SELECT title, subject
        INTO :TITLE, :SUBAREA:SINDIC
      FROM BOOK
     WHERE call_no = 100
END-EXEC.

IF SQLCODE = 0
    IF SINDIC = –1
        DISPLAY TITLE, " * * NULL * * "
    ELSE DISPLAY TITLE, SUBAREA
ELSE DISPLAY "BOOK WITH CALL_NO 100 NOT FOUND"
    DISPLAY "SQLCODE = * , SQLCODE.

Z100-LOG-ERROR.
    DISPLAY "INVALID USERNAME/PASSWORD".
    STOP RUN.

Z200-LOG-ERROR.
    DISPLAY "ERROR DISPLAYING CALL_NO = 100 ".
    DISPLAY SQLCODE.
    STOP RUN.
```

10
dBASE IV SQL

Ashton Tate's dBASE is a popular DBMS for the IBM-compatible microcomputers. The new release, dBASE IV supports the IBM SAA (Systems Application Architecture) standard for SQL. This enhancement is significant as it increases the visibility of dBASE in the professional database processing community.

This chapter covers various aspects of dBASE IV SQL. It describes the use of dBASE SQL in two modes — Interactive and Embedded. The Interactive mode is identical to working at the dot prompt. Database files are manipulated directly using SQL statements. The Embedded mode is used to develop application systems. It allows the creation of applications by SQL statements with a substantial subset of dBASE statements.

Because the original dBASE query language (called dBASE hereafter) is of interest to many, this chapter will compare it with Structured Query Language. Readers familiar with one of these languages can make an easy transition to the other. Various aspects of creating and manipulating a database are covered in both dBASE SQL and dBASE.

Examples are used extensively, and references are given to chapter 3, where they originally appeared. The examples will reveal that while certain queries can be implemented in both dBASE and SQL, one of the approaches will be more elegant than the other. A few SQL commands that have no comparable dBASE commands are identified. In dBASE, the semicolon (;) is used to indicate continuation of a query onto the next line. In SQL it is used only once — to mark the end of a query.

10.1 Starting dBASE SQL

It is recommended that the Protect utility in dBASE IV be invoked (using SQLDBA as the username) before you work with dBASE IV SQL. This way, the SQL catalog can keep track of the creators and users of tables. Commands such as **GRANT** and **REVOKE** can now be used meaningfully.

On starting dBASE, a screen asks for username and password. Once these are entered, you are in dBASE mode. When the Control Center appears, press **[ESC]** to display the dot prompt. Type **SET SQL ON**. This will take you into Interactive SQL mode. A SQL prompt will be visible from now on.

At the SQL prompt we can open an editing window by pressing **[Control]**-**[Home]**. A command may be typed on several lines, making it easy to read. Pressing the same keys again will close the window.

10.2 Creating a Database

Before a table is created or any SQL command is executed, we must create a database. We type the following command to create a database.

> **CREATE DATABASE** *database_name* ;

For example, we can type:

> **CREATE DATABASE** *LIBRARY*;

This will create a subdirectory called *LIBRARY* and the following message will be displayed by the system: *"Database LIBRARY created"*.

Several databases might reside on a given computer; therefore, a **START DATABASE** command has to be executed to indicate to dBASE IV which database (or catalog) is being activated. The command for activating a database is:

> **START DATABASE** *LIBRARY*;

Other useful commands are:

STOP DATABASE;	Closes the **LIBRARY** database
DROP DATABASE *LIBRARY*;	Erases the **LIBRARY** database
DROP TABLE BOOK;	Deletes the table BOOK
SHOW DATABASE;	Lists the databases

10.3 Creating a Table

All of the data definition statements, such as **CREATE TABLE**, and **DROP VIEW**, are available in dBASE SQL mode. Appendix B lists the SQL data definition statements. We now describe how the library database in figure 10.1 is created using both dBASE, and dBASE SQL (see chapter 2 for the case study). It is useful to point out here that dBASE IV (including dBASE SQL mode) does not support NULLs. Therefore, there is a difference in the library database definition in figure 10.2, when compared with the same in figure 2.1. (Also, the LOAN table in figure 2.1 is different from the LOAN table in figure 10.1, because a fine of 0.00 is stored automatically for each numeric data type with a NULL value.)

10.3.1 Creating a database in dBASE mode

The following steps will create the library database:

1. Type the **CREATE** command at the dot prompt, or select it in the **ASSIST** mode. Either way, dBASE IV displays a data definition screen that will be used to define the three tables depicted in figure 10.1.

Figure 10.1 Contents of tables in the Library database.

BOOK

call_no	title	subject
100	Physics Handbook	Physics
200	Database Systems	Computing
300	Modula-2	Computing
400	Database Design	Computing
500	Software Testing	Computing
600	Business Society	Business
700	Graphs	Mathematics
800	Cell Biology	Biology
900	Set Theory	Mathematics

LOAN

call_no	user_id	date_due	date_ret	fine	paid
100	100	09/12/88	09/01/88	0.00	
300	100	09/01/88	/ /	0.00	
900	200	01/01/88	12/20/88	1.90	yes
400	200	12/04/89	05/16/90	16.30	yes
600	200	12/04/89	05/16/90	16.30	yes
500	250	10/02/84	/ /	0.00	
600	250	10/02/84	10/02/85	36.50	yes
700	300	12/10/88	12/01/88	0.00	
800	350	12/01/88	12/30/88	2.90	yes
900	400	10/10/90	/ /	0.00	

PATRON

user_id	name	age
100	Wong	22
150	Colin	31
200	King	21
250	Das	67
300	Niall	17
350	Smith	72
400	Jones	41

2. Create BOOK.DBF:

Field Name	Type	Width	Dec
call_no	**NUMERIC**	3	0
title	**CHARACTER**	20	
subject	**CHARACTER**	12	

3. Append the book records (described in figure 10.1).

4. Create LOAN.DBF:

Field Name	Type	Width	Dec
call_no	**NUMERIC**	3	
user_id	**NUMERIC**	3	
date_due	**DATE**	8	
date_ret	**DATE**	8	
fine	**NUMERIC**	5	2
paid	**CHARACTER**	3	

5. Append the loan records (described in figure 10.1).

6. Finally, create PATRON.DBF:

Field Name	Type	Width	Dec
user_id	**NUMERIC**	3	0
name	**CHARACTER**	10	
age	**NUMERIC**	2	0

7. Append the patron records (described in figure 10.1).

10.3.2   Creating a Database in dBASE-SQL mode

To create the database in SQL mode we have two options. The first option is to use the **DBDEFINE** utility that comes with dBASE IV. The second option is to use the ANSI SQL **CREATE TABLE** command. The first option—using **DBDEFINE**—can only be used if the DBF files were created previously in dBASE mode. This is true here, and will be described next:

a)   Using DBDEFINE:

This approach can save you a lot of effort. **DBDEFINE** automatically creates catalog tables and entries for the current database. It loads the tables with data automatically from the current dBASE database. Let us create the **LIBRARY** database using **DBDEFINE**:

1. Create the **LIBRARY** database. Type:

    CREATE DATABASE *LIBRARY*;

2. Copy the files BOOK.DBF, LOAN.DBF and PATRON.DBF into the **LIBRARY** database directory. Use the **COPY** command for this purpose.

3. Activate the database by typing:

    START DATABASE *LIBRARY*;

4. Activate the utility **DBDEFINE** at the SQL prompt. Type:

    DBDEFINE

A message will be displayed if the above operation is successful. The utility creates a text file called DBDEFINE.TXT; and consists of several DDL statements generated by **DBDEFINE** while creating the tables, BOOK, LOAN, and PATRON.

b) Using the CREATE TABLE command:

The second option is to use the SQL data definition command **CREATE TABLE**. The commands described below are typed at the SQL prompt. Note that since dBASE IV does not support the NOT NULL option it is not used below:

```
SQL >      CREATE TABLE BOOK (
               call_no       NUMERIC(3),
               title         CHAR(20)
               subject       CHAR(12) );


SQL >      CREATE TABLE LOAN (
               call_no       NUMERIC(3),
               user_id       NUMERIC(3),
               date_due      DATE,
               date_ret      DATE,
               fine          NUMERIC(5,2),
               paid          CHAR(3) );


SQL >      CREATE TABLE PATRON (
               user_id       NUMERIC(3),
               name          CHAR(10),
               age           NUMERIC(2) );
```

Once the above tables have been defined, we can use the INSERT command to populate the tables. The following commands will load the BOOK table:

SQL> INSERT INTO book VALUES (100,"Physics Handbook","Physics");
SQL> INSERT INTO book VALUES (200,"Database Systems","Computing");
SQL> INSERT INTO book VALUES (300,"Modula-2","Computing");
SQL> INSERT INTO book VALUES (400,"Database Design","Computing");
SQL> INSERT INTO book VALUES (500,"Software Testing","Computing");
SQL> INSERT INTO book VALUES (600,"Business Society","Business");
SQL> INSERT INTO book VALUES (700,"Graphs","Mathematics");
SQL> INSERT INTO book VALUES (800,"Cell Biology","Biology");
SQL> INSERT INTO book VALUES (900,"Set Theory","Mathematics");

The loan records are inserted next into the **LOAN** table. Since dBASE IV does not support NULLs, the empty date_ret, fine, and paid fields should be defined as shown below:

SQL> INSERT INTO loan VALUES (100,100,{09/12/88},{09/01/88},0," ");
SQL> INSERT INTO loan VALUES (300,100,{09/01/88},{ / / },0," ");
SQL> INSERT INTO loan VALUES (900,200,{09/01/88},{12/20/88},1.90,"yes");
SQL> INSERT INTO loan VALUES 400,200,{12/04/89};{05/16/90},16.30,"yes");
SQL> INSERT INTO loan VALUES (600,200,{12/04/89},{05/16/90},16.30,"yes");
SQL> INSERT INTO loan VALUES (500,250,{10/02/84},{ / / },0," ");
SQL> INSERT INTO loan VALUES (600,250,{10/02/84},{10/02/85},36.50,"yes");
SQL> INSERT INTO loan VALUES 700,300,{12/10/88},{12/01/88},0," ");
SQL> INSERT INTO loan VALUES 800,350,{12/01/88},{12/30/88},2.90,"yes");
SQL> INSERT INTO loan VALUES (900,400,{10/01/90},{ / / },0," ");

Finally, the PATRON table is loaded in a similar manner:

SQL> INSERT INTO patron VALUES (100,"Wong",22);
SQL> INSERT INTO patron VALUES (150,"Colin",31);
SQL> INSERT INTO patron VALUES (200,"King",21);
SQL> INSERT INTO patron VALUES (250,"Das",67);
SQL> INSERT INTO patron VALUES (300,"Niall",17);
SQL> INSERT INTO patron VALUES (350,"Smith",72);
SQL> INSERT INTO patron VALUES (400,"Jones",41);

10.4 Retrieval Operations

The retrieval operations of dBASE SQL and dBASE are compared in this section starting with simple queries, qualified queries and partial match operators. Logical and arithmetic operators are covered next.

10.4.1 Simple queries

In SQL the **SELECT** command is primarily used to retrieve data from the database. It is also used with views and in conjunction with commands that update the database. This section concentrates on data retrieval.

Example: List all the data in the BOOK table.

dBASE SQL:	**SELECT** * **FROM** BOOK;
dBASE:	**USE BOOK** **LIST**

Result:	call_no	title	subject
	100	Physics Handbook	Physics
	200	Database Systems	Computing
	300	Modula-2	Computing
	400	Database Design	Computing
	500	Software Testing	Computing
	600	Business Society	Business
	700	Graphs	Mathematics
	800	Cell Biology	Biology
	900	Set Theory	Mathematics

In the SQL syntax described above, the * is used to display all the fields. The record numbers can be suppressed in dBASE by giving the command **LIST OFF** instead of **LIST**.

Example: List the title and subject for each book in the BOOK table.

dBASE SQL:	**SELECT** title, subject **FROM** BOOK
dBASE:	**USE BOOK** **LIST OFF** title, subject

Result:	title	subject
	Physics Handbook	Physics
	Database Systems	Computing
	Modula-2	Computing
	Database Design	Computing
	Software Testing	Computing
	Business Society	Business
	Graphs	Mathematics
	Cell Biology	Biology
	Set Theory	Mathematics

The **USE BOOK** command is not required in dBASE mode if the book table is active or open. But with SQL, no such assumption is made. Each query has to state which tables are being activated. This is done with the select command. The various tables are automatically closed at the end of the query.

Example: What are the subject areas of the library? (cf. ex. 3.4.)

dBASE SQL: **SELECT** subject
                 FROM BOOK;

dBASE: **USE BOOK**
             LIST OFF subject

Result:	subject
	Physics
	Computing
	Computing
	Computing
	Computing
	Business
	Mathematics
	Biology
	Mathematics

In the above result we have as many lines as there are books in the library. To remove redundancy, we can use the following commands:

dBASE SQL: **SELECT DISTINCT** subject
FROM BOOK;

dBASE: USE BOOK
INDEX ON subject **TO** subindex **UNIQUE**
LIST OFF subject

Result: **subject**

Physics
Computing
Business
Mathematics
Biology

dBASE requires us to use an index on the database before it will display unique subjects in the database. While this may not be an expedient approach (when compared to SQL's **DISTINCT** command) the dBASE query results in a sorted output (by subject): *Biology, Business, Computing, Mathematics*, and *Physics*.

Selecting rows from a single table

We now look at several examples used to retrieve rows from a table.

Example: List the title of mathematics books (cf. ex. 3.5).

dBASE SQL: **SELECT** title
FROM BOOK
WHERE subject = 'Mathematics';

dBASE:	USE BOOK
	LIST OFF title **FOR** subject = 'Mathematics'

Result:	title
	Graphs
	Set Theory

Using a **FOR** clause in dBASE will not work for **DATE** and **MEMO** fields. It is valid only for fields defined as **CHARACTER, NUMERIC,** or **LOGICAL** type. The date-to-character (**DTOC**) function should be used for the **DATE** type.

Example: List the book with call number 200 (cf. ex. 3.6).

dBASE SQL:	**SELECT** title
	FROM BOOK
	WHERE call_no = 200;

dBASE:	USE BOOK
	LIST OFF title **FOR** call_no = 200

Result:	call_no	title	subject
	200	Database Systems	Computing

In dBASE the **SET FILTER** clause can be used to eliminate the necessity of typing "**FOR** call_no = 200" repeatedly. The instruction "**SET FILTER TO** call_no = 200" followed by **LIST** is equivalent to the dBASE query illustrated above.

10.4.2   Arithmetic operators

The standard operators +, −, *, / are available for addition, subtraction, multiplication and division respectively.

Example: List patron fines in British pounds assuming one pound is equivalent to two dollars (cf. ex. 3.7).

dBASE SQL: **SELECT** call_no, user_id, fine*0.5
                  FROM LOAN;

dBASE: **USE** LOAN
                  LIST OFF call_no, user_id, fine*0.5

Result:

call_no	user_id	fine*0.5
100	100	
300	100	
900	200	0.95
400	200	8.15
600	200	8.15
500	250	
600	250	18.25
700	300	
800	350	1.45
900	400	

Example: List loans where the fine is over 10 British pounds (cf. ex. 3.8).

dBASE SQL: **SELECT** *
                  FROM LOAN
                  WHERE (fine*0.5) > 10.00;

dBASE: **USE** LOAN
                  LIST OFF FOR fine*0.5 > 10.00

Result:

call_no	user_id	date_due	date_ret	fine
600	250	10/02/84	10/02/85	36.50

10.4.3   Boolean operators

The above simple expressions can be used in logical expressions to form complex queries. Logical operators **AND, OR** and **NOT** expand search conditions. The priority of the Boolean operators from highest to lowest is **NOT, AND, OR**. Parentheses can be used to clarify or to force evaluation to be performed in a certain order.

Example: List the call numbers of books borrowed by patron number *200* or *250*, and where the fine paid is greater than $2.00 (cf. ex. 3.9).

dBASE SQL: SELECT call_no
FROM LOAN
WHERE fine > 2.00
AND (user_id=200 OR user_id=250)

dBASE: USE LOAN
LIST OFF call_no FOR (user_id = 200 .OR. user_id = 250)
.AND. fine > 2.00

Result: call_no

400

600

10.4.4 Special operators for the WHERE clause

There are four operators available in SQL to handle special cases: **LIKE, BETWEEN, IS NULL** and **IN.** (See chapter 3 for more details.) **LIKE** is used with character data to determine the presence of a substring. Special notations are available to specify unknown or irrelevant characters in the field being tested:

* a single unknown character: __ (underscore)
* any number of unknown characters: %

Example: List books that have the letters **"Database"** embedded in the title (cf. ex. 3.10).

dBASE SQL: SELECT
FROM BOOK
WHERE title LIKE '%Database%';

dBASE: USE BOOK
           LIST OFF FOR 'Database' $title

Result: | call_no | title | subject |
           |---------|------------------|-----------|
           | 200 | Database Systems | Computing |
           | 400 | Database Design | Computing |

In this example, the title field of each row in BOOK will be examined to determine if it contains the character string **"Database"**. Even though it is not evident here, books with titles such as *Design of Database Systems,* or *Databased Approach* will also be identified here.

Example: List books with titles having an *o* as the second character (cf. ex. 3.10).

dBASE SQL: **SELECT** *
               FROM BOOK
               WHERE title **LIKE** '_ o % ';

dBASE: USE* BOOK
               LIST OFF FOR SUBSTR(title,2,1) = 'o'

Result: | call_no | title | subject |
           |---------|------------------|-----------|
           | 300 | Modula-2 | Computing |
           | 500 | Software Testing | Computing |

Since dBASE does not have the **LIKE** command, the **SUBSTR**ing function is used instead to obtain the same result.

10.4.5 BETWEEN

The **BETWEEN** operator is used with numeric data to determine if a field lies in a certain range.

Example: List books with call numbers between 200 and 400 (cf. ex. 3.12).

dBASE SQL: SELECT *
         FROM BOOK
         WHERE call_no BETWEEN 200 AND 400;

dBASE: USE BOOK
           LIST OFF FOR (call_no > = 200) AND. (call_no < = 400)

Result:	call_no	title	subject
	200	Database Systems	Computing
	300	Modula-2	Computing
	400	Database Design	Computing

dBASE does not have the **BETWEEN** operator; consequently the **FOR** command is used with .AND. to obtain the same results.

10.4.6   IS NULL

NULL is a key word that must be used to determine whether or not a field has been assigned a value. Note that in our database, the *date returned* field is not assigned a value until a book is returned. If a book is returned on time, no value is assigned to the *fine* field.

Example: List the books currently out on loan (cf. ex. 3.13).

Unlike Standard SQL, dBASE IV SQL does not support the **NULL** expression. Consequently, the SQL query has to be modified as illustrated:

SQL Standard: SELECT call_no
                FROM LOAN
                WHERE date_ret IS NULL;

dBASE SQL: SELECT call_no
                FROM LOAN
                WHERE DTOC(date_ret) - " / / ";

dBASE: USE LOAN
                LIST call_no FOR DTOC(date_ret) = " / / "

Result: **call_no**

300

500

900

The desired results are obtained in dBASE mode by using blanks within quotes. **DTOC** converts **DATE** type to **CHARACTER** type. Using three or more blanks will not display desired results, but two blanks will work.

Example: List the books that have been returned by user 100 (cf. ex. 3.14).

dBASE SQL: **SELECT** call_no
FROM LOAN
WHERE (user_id=100)
AND DTOC(date_ret) < > " / / "

dBASE: **USE** LOAN
LIST OFF call_no **WHERE** user_id=100
AND DTOC(date_ret) < > " / / "

Result: **call_no**

100

This is similar to the previous query but a 'not equal' symbol (< >) is used.

10.4.7   IN

The set of values used for comparison can be either explicitly specified or given as a subquery. We illustrate the first case here and leave subqueries for a later section.

Example: List the names of patrons whose *user_id is* 100, 200, 300, or 350 (cf. ex. 3.15).

dBASE SQL: **SELECT** name
                FROM USER
                WHERE user_id **IN** (100,200,300,350);

dBASE: **USE** name
                LIST OFF name **FOR** user_id = 100
                .OR. user_id = 200
                .OR. user_id = 300
                .OR. user_id = 350

Result: **name**
                Wong
                King
                Niall
                Smith

Since dBASE does not have the **IN** command, the equivalent query is lengthy and can be very tedious.

Example: List all computing and history titles (cf. ex. 3.16).

dBASE SQL: **SELECT** title
              FROM BOOK
              WHERE subject **IN** ('Computing', 'History');

dBASE: USE BOOK
              LIST OFF title **FOR** subject = 'Computing'
              .OR. subject = 'History'

Result: **title**

              Database Systems
              Modula-2
              Database Design
              Software Testing

10.4.8 Use of system variables

SQL systems use system variables used to hold values of general use or interest (refer to chapter 3.6). In dBASE SQL the current date can be obtained by using **DATE( )**.

Example: List patrons who have outstanding books as of the current date. Assume today is September 13, 1990 (cf. ex. 3.17).

dBASE SQL: SELECT user_id
FROM LOAN
WHERE DTOC(date_ret) = " / / "
AND DATE( ) > date_due

dBASE: USE LOAN
LIST OFF user_id FOR DTOC(date_ret) = ' / / '
.AND. DATE( ) > date_due

Result: user_id

100
250

The **DATE( )** function is used to obtain the current date in both dBASE and dBASE SQL.

10.4.9 Column functions

SQL offers special aggregate functions to determine maximums, minimums, averages, totals and counts for entire columns. These are **MAX, MIN, AVG, SUM,** and **COUNT** respectively.

Example: What is the largest fine paid for an overdue book? (cf. ex. 3.18).

dBASE SQL: SELECT MAX(fine)
               FROM LOAN;

dBASE: USE LOAN
               mfine = fine
               DO WHILE .NOT. EOF( )
                      mfine = MAX(mfine,fine)
                      SKIP
               ENDDO
               ? mfine

Result: max(fine)
               36.50

While the SQL query is elegant and requires little explanation, the dBASE query is wearisome. It involves the following components: a *loop*, **DO WHILE.NOT**.end Of File . . . **ENDDO**; a **MAX** function; and finally a **SKIP** statement which skips a record at a time. The last step is a question mark (?) which is equivalent to saying "print the value of the variable *mfine*."

Example: How much has the library assessed in fines? (cf. ex. 3.19.)

dBASE SQL: SELECT SUM(fine)
               FROM LOAN;

dBASE: USE LOAN
               SUM fine TO tfine
               ? tfine

               OR

               USE LOAN
               SUM fine

Result: sum(fine)
               73.90

The first of these dBASE queries stores the total fine into a variable called *tfine*, and then displays the results of this query. The second query directly displays the same results.

10.4.10 Use of DISTINCT

SQL mode permits the specification of **DISTINCT** with an aggregate function; the effect is to remove duplicate values prior to the function being applied.

Example: How many subject area are there? (cf. ex. 3.23.)

dBASE SQL: SELECT COUNT(DISTINCT subject)
            FROM BOOK;

dBASE: USE BOOK
            INDEX ON subject **TO** subindex **UNIQUE**
            COUNT

  Result: **count(distinct subject)**

            5

The dBASE example, once again, makes use of the **INDEX** operation to obtain the desired results. If the index SUBINDEX already exists we give the following command: **USE BOOK INDEX** SUBINDEX" followed by **COUNT**. Whenever **DISTINCT** is used, the argument must be a simple field reference such as *subject* used above.

10.4.12 Use of *

COUNT can take * as an argument, and therefore can be used to count the number of rows involved for some query.

Example: How many computing books are there in the
            library? (cf. ex. 3.22.)

dBASE SQL: **SELECT COUNT(*)**
                 FROM BOOK
                 WHERE subject = 'Computing';

dBASE: **USE** BOOK
                 COUNT FOR subject = 'Computing'

Result: **count(*)**

                 4

10.4.13 ORDERing the result

The **ORDER BY** clause is used to force the result to be ordered by one or more column values in either ascending or descending order.

Example: List books in alphabetical order by title (cf. ex. 3.25).

dBASE SQL: **SELECT** *
                 FROM BOOK
                 ORDER BY title;

dBASE: **USE** BOOK
                 INDEX ON title **TO** bktitle
                 LIST OFF

Result:	call_no	title	subject
	600	Business Society	Business
	800	Cell Biology	Biology
	400	Database Design	Computing
	200	Database Systems	Computing
	700	Graphs	Mathematics
	300	Modula-2	Computing
	100	Physics Handbook	Physics
	900	Set Theory	Mathematics
	500	Software Testing	Computing

The dBASE query uses the **INDEX** operation to provide the desired results. A SORT command is also available in dBASE to provide similar results, but it creates a new table with ordered records.

Example: List books in subject order; and within subject, order them by call number in descending order (cf. ex. 3.26).

dBASE SQL: **SELECT** *
                  FROM BOOK
                  ORDER BY subject **ASC**, call_no **DESC**;

dBASE: USE BOOK
                  SORT ON subject/**A**, call_no/D **TO** subcall
                  USE SUBCALL
                  LIST OFF

Result:	call_no	title	subject
	800	Cell Biology	Biology
	600	Business Society	Business
	500	Software Testing	Computing
	400	Database Design	Computing
	300	Modula-2	Computing
	200	Database Systems	Computing
	900	Set Theory	Mathematics
	700	Graphs	Mathematics
	100	Physics Handbook	Physics

Note that the result is ordered first by subject and within each subject by descending *call_no*. The dBASE query requires us to create a new database file called **SUBCALL** in order to achieve the same results. This is not a desirable situation, as it introduces a redundant table in our database.

It would have been appropriate to use the **INDEX** command as illustrated in the previous example, but this does not provide us the desired results. The **INDEX** command has **ASC**ending and **DESC**ending ordering options, but both cannot be used in the same index expression.

10.4.14 Join

The **JOIN** operation is used to retrieve information from more than one table (see chapter 3 for more information). In order to retrieve information from more than two tables, the **SELECT** and **SET RE-LATION TO** clause are used. Refer to the example for more details.

Note: dBASE has a **JOIN** keyword; it is, however, used differently. It creates a new target table by combining two source tables. The effects of the **JOIN** command are permanent, and dBASE **JOIN** is not used or discussed in this book. The following examples describe how information can be obtained from two or more tables concurrently.

Example: List the names of *patrons* their *user_id*'s, and the call numbers of the books they have borrowed (cf. ex. 3.31). Here we have to use two tables to get the information: PATRON and LOAN. What we need to do is specify that a row of PATRON should be matched with a row of LOAN whenever they have the same value for the *user_id* field. Note that one row of PATRON can be matched with many rows of LOAN since a patron is expected to borrow many books. With SQL it is necessary for us to specify this **JOIN** condition explicitly.

dBASE SQL: **SELECT** patron.name, patron.user_id, loan.call_no
FROM PATRON, LOAN
WHERE patron.user_id = loan.user_id;

dBASE: **USE** PATRON
INDEX ON user_id **TO** USER_ID

(Indexing is done only once)

SELECT 2
USE PATRON **INDEX** USER_ID
SELECT 1
USE LOAN
SET RELATION TO user_id **INTO** PATRON
LIST OFF patron $\rightarrow$ name, user_id, call_no

Result:	patron.name	patron.user_id	loan.call_no
	Wong	100	100
	Wong	100	300
	King	200	900
	King	200	400
	King	200	600
	Das	250	500
	Das	250	600
	Niall	300	700
	Smith	350	800
	Jones	400	900

The dBASE query is relatively complex. To begin with, the common field *user_id* has to be indexed prior to employing the **SET RELATION TO** command. dBASE IV permits up to 10 open files. The **SELECT** clause is used to designate work areas. Numbers 1 to 10, (or A to J) are used to store open files. The **USE** command is utilized to assign a file to an opened work area. Since only one file can be active at any given time, the " —> " symbol is open to open a file that is not active.

In the dBASE example above, the PATRON file is allocated to work *area 2* with the command **SELECT 2**. The LOAN file is allocated to work *area 1*. The command: "**SET RELATION TO** *user_id* **INTO** PATRON", links the two tables via their common field *user_id*. Note that in order to **LIST** the names, we must use the command "**LIST OFF** PATRON –> NAME". The " –> " symbol points to the *name* column in the PATRON table. Needless to say, the SQL approach to joining files and obtaining information from multiple tables is much simpler.

Example: List the names of patrons who have books out on loan (cf. ex. 3.32). The information needed to do this is found in two tables: LOAN contains the record of books loaned out (specifically we are interested in those rows where the *date_ret* column has no value) and PATRON contains the *name* and *age* for each patron. We need to match up a selected row of LOAN with the related row of PATRON; this is done by requiring them to have the same value for the *user_id* field.

dBASE SQL: SELECT name
FROM LOAN, PATRON
WHERE loan.date_ret IS NULL
AND loan.user_id = patron.user_id;

dBASE: USE PATRON
INDEX ON user_id TO USER_ID
SELECT 2
USE PATRON INDEX USER_ID
SELECT 1
USE LOAN
SET RELATION TO user_id INTO PATRON
LIST OFF PATRON –> name WHERE date_ret = " / / "

Result: patron.name

Wong
Das
Jones

Example: List each patron's name and the number of patrons older than he/she (cf. ex. 3.33).

SQL: SELECT a.name, COUNT(*)
FROM PATRON a, PATRON b
WHERE a.age < b.age
GROUP BY a.user_id, a.name;

We obtain the results as displayed in ex. 3.33.

The above SQL query will not work in either mode if it is structured as follows:

SQL: SELECT a.name, COUNT(*)
FROM PATRON a, PATRON b
WHERE a.age < b.age
GROUP BY a.user_id

It is possible, however, to obtain partial results in dBASE SQL mode by omitting the **COUNT(*)** statement as follows:

dBASE SQL: **SELECT** a.name
FROM PATRON a, PATRON b
WHERE a.age < b.age
GROUP BY a.user_id

This query will simply provide results as follows: Only the names are listed; the name *Wong* will appear four times, the name *Colin* will appear three times, the name *King* will appear five times, . . . ; this is equivalent to the results provided by **COUNT(*)** in SQL.

10.5 Updating the Database

In dBASE SQL, there are three commands for updating the database:

1. **UPDATE** modifies rows of tables
2. **DELETE** removes rows from tables
3. **INSERT** adds new rows to tables

Views cannot be updated in dBASE IV, only individual tables.
The dBASE mode supports the above three operations with the following commands:

1. **REPLACE** modifies rows of tables
2. **DELETE** followed by **PACK** removes rows from tables
3. **INSERT** or **APPEND** adds new rows to tables

dBASE IV is a full fledged DBMS and therefore has several additional commands to support data entry and updating operations, such as **BROWSE, EDIT** and **CHANGE.** They are available in dBASE mode only and not in the dBASE SQL mode.

Modifying existing rows

Example: Increase every patrons age by 10.

    dBASE SQL: **UPDATE** PATRON
                              SET age = age + 10;

    dBASE: **USE** PATRON
                              REPLACE age **WITH** age + 10

Note that since there is no conditional clause (**WHERE** in SQL and **FOR** in dBASE), every row of PATRON is modified.

Example: Determine fines. In this example we want to modify only those rows of LOAN which meet the criteria:

    a) the *fine* field is **NULL** (or has a value of 0.00 dollars)
    b) the book has been returned
    c) the book was overdue

dBASE SQL: **UPDATE** LOAN
                         SET fine = (date_ret − date_due) * 0.10
                         WHERE fine = 0
                         AND date_ret > date_due;

dBASE: **USE** LOAN
                         REPLACE fine **WITH** ((date_ret − date_due) * 0.10)
                         FOR fine = 0
                         AND date_ret > date_due;

Deleting rows

The **DELETE** command can be used to delete selected rows from a table; the rows deleted are those that satisfy the condition specified in the **WHERE** clause. The **WHERE** clause is *optional*; if absent then all rows are deleted.

Example: Delete all the Physics books from the BOOK table.

SQL: **DELETE FROM** BOOK
                WHERE subject = 'Physics';

dBASE: **USE** BOOK
                DELETE FOR subject = 'Physics'

It should be noted that in dBASE, the delete command only marks the record for deletion; it may be recovered by typing the command **RECALL . ALL** . To purge the records permanently, the command **PACK** is given following **DELETE.**

Example: Remove all loan records for patron *Smith*.

dBASE SQL: **DELETE FROM** LOAN
                WHERE user_id =
                (**SELECT** user_id
                FROM PATRON
                WHERE name = 'Smith');

dBASE: **USE** PATRON
                INDEX ON user_id **TO** USERID
                SELECT 2
                USE PATRON **INDEX** USERID
                SELECT 1
                USE LOAN
                SET RELATION TO user_id **INTO** B
                DELETE FOR B – > name = 'Smith'
                PACK

Inserting new rows

dBASE provides you an **APPEND** command and **BROWSE** command to insert rows into a table.

Example: Add a new patron to the database.

dBASE SQL: **INSERT INTO** PATRON (user_id, name, age)
VALUES (900, 'Jones',35);

dBASE: **USE** PATRON
APPEND (You enter above values when
prompted)

Deleting tables

Deleting tables is different from deleting rows.

Example: Remove the table OLDBOOKS; we no longer need
it.

dBASE SQL: **DROP TABLE** OLDBOOKS;

dBASE: **ERASE** OLDBOOKS.DBF

10.6 Embedded dBASE SQL

The Embedded SQL mode allows us to create application programs
and menu-driven systems. If there are sequences of SQL statements
that have to be executed frequently, it is better to create a program.
We explain the use of SQL using the dBASE programming language
as the host language. It is assumed that you are familiar with chapter
8 which provides an overview of application programming using
Embedded SQL statements, and that you are familiar with dBASE
programming constructs such as **DO . . . ENDDO**, and **IF . . .
ENDIF**.

You will notice some differences when Embedded dBASE SQL
programming is compared with COBOL or PL/I SQL programming. The most prominent is that no **EXEC SQL** and **END EXEC**
statements are required.

10.6.1 Creating a program

In order to create an Embedded SQL program, use the command:

MODIFY COMMAND filename.prs

The *prs* extension after the file name is very important; otherwise the program is treated as a dBASE program, executing it outside the SQL mode and excluding all SQL commands.

To save the program, press the keys **[CNTRL-END]**; and to compile, enter

COMPILE filename.prs

To execute the program enter

DO filename

Several programs are discussed in this section to illustrate Embedded SQL. Table 10.1 below lists all of them and provides a brief description of their capabilities.

Table 10.1 Embedded dBASE Programs

Program Number	Program Name	Program Description
1	Book_Ret	Retrieves a book
2	Book_Ins	Inserts a new book
3	MBook_Ins	Inserts many books
4	FineList	Lists the fines due for all patrons
5	JoinFine	Lists fines in ascending order
6	Fines	Calculates fine & updates table
7	MBook_Del	Deletes books
8	M_Cursors	Illustrates use of several cursors

10.6.2 Embedded SQL without CURSORs

Conceptually, the SQL **CURSOR** is equivalent to a record pointer in dBASE. And like the record pointer, it can be moved from one row to another through the table. A **CURSOR** is used extensively in SQL programming, but we can get by without it if we do not need to access the rows individually. Program 1 describes such a situation in the context of the BOOK table. It describes how we can retrieve and display a book.

The **INTO** clause (see program 1) is used to direct output of the *book_retrieve* query away from the screen and into the memory variables *mcall_no, mtitle,* and *msubject.*

Program 1:   Retrieve a book from the book table.

MODIFY COMMAND book_ret.prs

On typing the above command we enter an editor where the following code is typed. Statements that follow an asterisk are remark statements and serve to document the program.

*********************start of program*********************

```
* Program Name: book_ret.prs
* Initialize the variables mcall_no, mtitle and msubject.

STORE 0 TO mcall_no
STORE SPACE(20) TO mtitle
STORE SPACE(12) TO msubject
CLEAR

* Input book call number from screen and store into variable.
* The @ command positions the cursor.

@5,25 SAY " BOOK RETRIEVAL SCREEN "
@6,25 SAY " *_____ "
@9,5 SAY " PLEASE ENTER CALL NUMBER OF DESIRED BOOK: " GET
mcall_no
READ
```

```
* Book retrieval embedded statements

SELECT call_no, title, subject
INTO mcall_no, mtitle, msubject
FROM BOOK
WHERE call_no = mcall_no;

* Book display statements
* The CLEAR command clears the screen for display.
CLEAR

@5,25 SAY " BOOK INFORMATION "
@6,25 SAY " ——————————— "
@9,10 SAY " Book Call Number: " GET mcall_no
@11,10 SAY " Title of Book: " GET mtitle
@13,10 SAY " Book Subject: " GET msubject
```

********************end of program*********************

Save the program using [CNTRL]-[END], compile it, and execute it with the command:

    DO book_Ret.prs

On running the above program we see a screen prompting us for the call number of a book:

```
┌──────────────────────────────────────────────┐
│                                                │
│     BOOK RETRIEVAL SCREEN                      │
│     – – – – – – – – – – – – – –                │
│                                                │
│   PLEASE ENTER CALL NUMBER OF DESIRED BOOK:    │
│                                                │
└──────────────────────────────────────────────┘
```

On typing 100 we obtain the following results:

BOOK INFORMATION
— — — — — — — — — —
Book Call Number: 100
Title of Book: Physics Handbook
Book Subject: Physics

Program 2: Create a program that will insert a new book
into the table.

This program will insert a new book into the BOOK table. It
simplifies the data manipulation operation considerably and makes
it less tedious.

To create the program type:

MODIFY COMMAND book_ins.prs

********************start of program*********************

* Initialize the variables mcall_no, mtitle and msubject.

STORE 0 TO mcall_no
STORE SPACE(20) **TO** mtitle
STORE SPACE(12) **TO** msubject

CLEAR

* Read data from the screen and store into variables

@5,10 **SAY** " BOOK ENTRY SCREEN "
@6,10 **SAY** "— — — — — — — — — — —"
@9,5 **SAY** "CALL NUMBER: " **GET** mcall_no
@11,5 **SAY** "BOOK TITLE: " **GET** mtitle
@13,5 **SAY** "BOOK SUBJECT: " **GET** msubject
READ

* Embedded SQL statement to insert a record

INSERT INTO BOOK
VALUES (mcall_no, mtitle, msubject);

*********************end of program*********************

Once again save, compile and execute the program. The following screen appears on running the program.

```
BOOK ENTRY SCREEN
- - - - - - - - - - - -
CALL NUMBER:
BOOK TITLE:
BOOK SUBJECT:
```

Enter the following data:

```
BOOK ENTRY SCREEN
- - - - - - - - - - -
CALL NUMBER:        999
BOOK TITLE:         A Guide to DB2
BOOK SUBJECT:       Computing
```

The above book is now stored into the BOOK table. You can verify that by typing **"SELECT * FROM** BOOK;" at the "SQL >" prompt.

Program 3: Create a program that will insert several books into the table.

This program is almost identical to the previous program, except that the previous program inserts a single book into the table and stops. Program 3 will permit you to add several books; it stops when you say No to the prompt, "Add Another Book?". This program also illustrates how Embedded SQL can be used to load a table after it has been created.

You may want to modify or copy the above program to mbook_in.prs to avoid retyping it. Then type:

MODIFY COMMAND mbook_ins.prs

********************start of program********************

```
* program name:mbook_ins.prs
* Open a Loop

DO WHILE .T.
* Initialize the variables mcall_no, mtitle, and msubject.
STORE 0 TO mcall_no
STORE SPACE(20) TO mtitle
STORE SPACE(12) TO msubject
CLEAR

* Read data from the screen and store into variables

@5,10 SAY " BOOK ENTRY SCREEN "
@6,10 SAY " - - - - - - - - - - "
@9,5 SAY "CALL NUMBER: " GET mcall_no
@11,5 SAY "BOOK TITLE: " GET mtitle
@13,5 SAY "BOOK SUBJECT: " GET msubject
READ

* Return if blank entry
IF mcall_no = 0
        RETURN
ENDIF
```

* embedded SQL statement to insert record

INSERT INTO BOOK
VALUES (mcall_no, mtitle, msubject);

* The **PICTURE "!"** will convert input to upper case.

reply = "N"
@ 16,5 **SAY** "Add another book? [Type Y/N]";
      GET reply **PICTURE "!"**
READ

IF reply = "N"
      RETURN
ENDIF
* End the loop
ENDDO

********************end of program*********************

10.6.3 Program illustrating use of a CURSOR

So far we avoided using the **CURSOR**, but the next few examples will illustrate the use of one. To employ **CURSOR**s we need four command verbs:

      DECLARE   Sets up the cursor

        OPEN   Makes rows available via a cursor

       FETCH   Increments the cursor location and transfers data into memory variables.

       CLOSE   Closes a cursor. When it is reopened it points to the first row of the table.

Program 4:   Display the fines due for all patrons.

This program displays fines due for all the patrons in ascending order by fines (i.e., smallest fine to largest fine). This is accomplished by the "**ORDER BY** fine" clause. The system variable SQLCODE is used to test the results of a SQL statement. If the command is successful SQLCODE has a value of 0. It has a negative value if an error occurs. If a **FETCH** is issued when the **CURSOR** points beyond the last row, SQLCODE will have a value of + 100.

Type a new program called Finelist.prs:

MODIFY COMMAND finelist.prs

********************start of program********************

```
* Program Name: Finelist.prs
* Initialize the variables mcall_no, mtitle and msubject.

STORE 0 TO mcall_no
STORE 0 TO muser_id
STORE 0 TO mfine
CLEAR

* The select statement retrieves records that have a fine.

DECLARE fines_cr CURSOR FOR
        SELECT call_no, user_id, fine
        FROM LOAN
        WHERE fine > 0
        ORDER BY fine;

OPEN fines_cr ;
```

```
DO WHILE .T.
          FETCH fines_cr INTO mcall_no, muser_id, mfine;

                    * If no rows returned by FETCH, close cursor
                    and quit

                    IF SQLCODE > = 100
                              CLOSE fines_cr;
                              RETURN
                              ENDIF

          CLEAR
          @10,10 SAY "Patron ID: " + STR(muser_id)
          @12,10 SAY "Call Number: " + STR(mcall_no)
          @14,10 SAY "Fine Due: $" + STR(mfine,5,2)
          ?
          ?
          WAIT

ENDDO
```

*********************end of program*********************

On executing the program we see five screens displaying fines ranging from $1.90 (for user_id 200) to $ 36.50 (for user_id 250). Only the first screen is shown below:

Patron ID: 200

Call Number: 900

Fine Due: $ 1.90

press any key to continue.

Program 5: Display the fines due from all patrons in ascending order by name. This program is similar to Program 5, but it illustrates the use of **CURSORs** in the context of a **JOIN**. Two tables have to be joined in order to obtain the results.

*********************start of program*********************

* This program lists *fines* due for all the patrons in ascending order of name.

* It illustrates how two tables can be joined while using **CURSORs**

* Program Name: JoinFine.prs

* Initialize the variables

STORE 0 **TO** mcall_no
STORE 0 **TO** muser_id
STORE 0 **TO** mfine
STORE SPACE(10) **TO** mname
CLEAR

* The **SELECT** statement retrieves only those records that have
* a fine.

DECLARE fines_cr **CURSOR FOR**
       SELECT loan.call_no, loan.user_id, loan.fine, patron.name
       FROM LOAN, PATRON
       WHERE fine > 0
       AND loan.user_id = patron.user_id
       ORDER BY patron.name;

OPEN fines_cr ;

DO WHILE .T.
       FETCH fines.cr **INTO** mcall_no, muser_id, mfine, mname;

* If no rows returned by **FETCH** then close cursor and quit

```
IF SQLCODE > = 100
        CLOSE fines_cr;
        RETURN
ENDIF


CLEAR
@8,10 SAY "Patron ID: " + STR(muser_id)
@10,10 SAY "Patron Name: " + mname
@12,10 SAY "Call Number: " + STR (mcall_no)
@14,10 SAY "Fine Due: $" + STR (mfine,5,2)
?
?
WAIT


ENDDO
```

*******************end of program*********************

On executing Program 5, we once again see five screens, this time in order of patron names ranging from Das (**user_id** 250) to Smith (**user_id** 350). The first screen is shown:

Patron ID: 250

Patron Name: Das

Call Number: 600

Fine Due: $36.50

press any key to continue.

Program 6:   Calculate fines for all patrons and store the results in the **fine** column of LOAN table.

Such a program would ideally be executed every day, before the library opens. It updates all records that have a fine due. There is no visible output (on screen or paper) when the program is executed, it simply calculates the fine for each overdue book at $ 0.10 per day and updates the loan table.

This program also illustrates the use of **CURSOR**'s **FOR UP-DATE**ing. The syntax for opening a cursor is:

> **DECLARE** cursor_name **CURSOR**
> **FOR SELECT**-statements
> **FOR UPDATE OF** column-list

In the program below, the column list contains **fine**. The syntax for **UPDATE WHERE CURRENT OF** is as follows:

> **UPDATE** table_name
> **SET** column_name=expression, . . .
> **WHERE CURRENT OF** cursor_name

To create the following program type the command:

> **MODIFY COMMAND** fines.prs

********************start of program********************

```
* Program Name: Fines.prs
* This program calculates fines for all patrons. It updates the
* loan table with fines due.

* Initialize the variables mcall_no, mtitle and msubject.

STORE 0 TO mcall_no
STORE 0 TO muser_id
STORE "  /  /  " TO mdate_due
STORE "  /  /  " TO  mdate_ret
```

```
STORE 0 TO mfine
CLEAR


* Retrieval of books – embedded statements
*
* The select statement retrieves only those records that are
* eligible for a fine.
*
* It is necessary to filer records that have already paid a fine
* and hence the clause "WHERE FINE = 0"

DECLARE fincs_cr CURSOR FOR
            SELECT call_no, user_id, date_due, date_ret, fine
            FROM LOAN
            WHERE fine = 0
            AND date_ret > date_due
            FOR UPDATE OF fine;


OPEN fines_cr ;

DO WHILE .T.
            FETCH fincs_cr INTO mcall_no, muser_id, mdate_due,
            mdate_ret. mfine;

            * If no rows returned by FETCH then close cursor and quit

            IF SQLCODE > = 100
                CLOSE fines_cr;
                RETURN
            ENDIF

            * Update records with fines at $ 0.10 a day.

            UPDATE LOAN
            SET fine = (date_ret - date_due) * 0.10
            WHERE CURRENT OF fines_cr;

ENDDO
```

********************end of program********************

Program 7: Delete the book, *Physics Handbook* (*call_no* 100); and the book, *A Guide to DB2* (*call_no* 999).

This program illustrates useful programming techniques. A book is deleted only after it is displayed on the screen (and delete is allowed by the user). It also asks you if more books have to be deleted; if so, the entire process is repeated once again.

*********************start of program*********************

* Program Name: Mbookdel.prs

* This program illustrates the use of a LOOP in deleting
* several books. It displays the book and deletes it
* after verification from user.

DO WHILE .T.

       * Initialize the variables mcall_no, mtitle and msubject.

       STORE 0 **TO** mcall_no
       STORE SPACE(20) **TO** mtitle
       STORE SPACE(12) **TO** msubject

       CLEAR

       * Input Call Number of book to be deleted
       @ 10,10 **SAY** "Enter Call Number of book to be deleted" ;
           GET mcall_no
       READ

       * Stop routine

       IF mcall_no = 0
           RETURN
       ENDIF

```
DECLARE call_cr CURSOR FOR
     SELECT call_no, title, subject
     FROM BOOK
     WHERE call_no = mcall_no
FOR UPDATE OF call_no, title, subject
OPEN call_cr;

FETCH call_cr INTO mcall_no, mtitle, msubject;

* No record found

IF SQLCODE > = 100
     ? " Book not found in database, try again"
     ?
     WAIT
     LOOP
ENDIF

CLEAR

* Read data from book table and store into variables

@5,10 SAY " BOOK DELETE SCREEN "
@6,10 SAY " - - - - - - - - - - - - "

@9,5 SAY "CALL NUMBER: " + STR(mcall_no)
@11,5 SAY "BOOK TITLE: " + mtitle
@13,5 SAY "BOOK SUBJECT: " + MSUBJECT

reply1 = "N"
@ 16,5 SAY " Delete this book? [Type Y/N] " ;
GET reply1 PICTURE "!"
READ

IF reply1 = "Y"
     DELETE FROM BOOK
     WHERE CURRENT OF call_cr;
ENDIF
```

```
        CLOSE call_cr;

        CLEAR

        * Stop routine
        reply2 = "N"

        @ 16,5 SAY "Delete another book? [Type Y/N] " ;
        GET reply2*PICTURE "!"
        READ

        IF reply2 = "N"
              RETURN
        ENDIF

        * End the loop

ENDDO
```

********************end of program********************

On executing the program we are presented with the following screen:

```
┌─────────────────────────────────────────────────────────┐
│                                                           │
│                                                           │
│  Enter Call Number of book to be deleted:                 │
│                                                           │
│                                                           │
└─────────────────────────────────────────────────────────┘
```

In response to the above prompt enter the call number 100.

BOOK DELETE SCREEN
– – – – – – – – – – –
Book Call Number: 100
Title of Book: Physics Handbook
Book Subject: Physics

Delete this book? [Type Y/N]

On typing in Y, the book will be deleted from the table. You will then see the prompt:

Delete another book? [Type Y/N]

On typing Y the program LOOPS again. You exit from the program when you respond N (No) to the same prompt.

10.6.4   Using more than one CURSOR

So far we did not have more than one CURSOR open at any given time. In several cases, you may not need to do so either. You will however, find it useful to have more than one cursor open if you have to inspect all the values (or update) in another table on the basis of the values in the former. This is illustrated in the program MCURSORS.PRS below.

Program 8:   Calculate the new fines due for all senior patrons (aged sixty and higher) if they are fined at a reduced rate based on the table below.

If the old *fine* (as displayed in the LOAN table in Table 3.1) is between $0 and $5, the *newfine* is $0. If the old *fine* is between $40 and $50, the *newfine* is $13.

oldfine1	oldfine2	newfine
0	5	0.00
5	10	2.00
10	15	5.00
15	20	7.00
20	25	9.00
25	30	10.00
30	40	11.11
40	50	13.00

In order to implement the above program you will first have to create a table called SIXTYPLS and define the three columns *oldfine1*, *oldfine2* and *newfine*. Insert the values displayed above into the table. Now type in the program below:

MODIFY COMMAND mcursors.prs

********************start of program*********************

```
* Program Name: Mcursors.prs
* This program lists fines due for all the patrons in ascending
* order of name.
* Seniors are fined at a reduced rate (based on SIXTYPLS table).
* Two cursors are used: SENIORS and FINES_CR.
* Initialize the variables mcall_no, mtitle and msubject.

STORE 0 TO mcall_no
STORE 0 TO muser_id
STORE 0 TO mfine
STORE SPACE(10) TO mname
STORE 0 TO mage
```

```
STORE 0 TO moldfin1
STORE 0 TO moldfin2
STORE 0 TO mnewfine
CLEAR


* The select statement retrieves only those tuples that have
* a fine.

DECLARE fines_cr CURSOR FOR
        SELECT loan.call_no, loan.user_id, loan.fine, patron.name, patron.age
        FROM LOAN, PATRON
        WHERE fine > 0
        AND loan.user_id = patron.user_id
        ORDER BY patron.name;

DECLARE seniors CURSOR FOR
        SELECT oldfine1, oldfine2, newfine
        FROM SixtyPls;


* Opens first cursor

OPEN fines_cr ;

DO WHILE .T.
        FETCH fines_cr INTO mcall_no, muser_id, mfine, mname, mage;

            * If no rows returned by FETCH then close cursor and quit

            IF SQLCODE > = 100
                CLOSE fines_cr;
                RETURN
            ENDIF

        IF mage > 65

        *opens second cursor
        OPEN SENIORS;

        DO WHILE SQLCODE < 100
```

```
        FETCH SENIORS INTO moldfin1, moldfin2, mnewfine;
            IF SQLCODE > = 100
                CLOSE seniors;
                RETURN
            ENDIF

            IF mfine > moldfin1
                IF mfine < moldfin2
                mfine = mnewfine
                SQLCODE = 100
                CLOSE seniors;
                ENDIF
            ENDIF
        ENDDO

    ENDIF

    CLEAR
    @8,20 SAY "Patron ID: ' + STR(muser_id)
    @10,10 SAY "Patron Name " + mname
    @12,10 SAY "Call Number: " + STR(mcall_no)
    @14,10 SAY "Fine Due: $" + STR(mfine,5,2)
    ?
    ?
    WAIT

ENDDO

********************end of program*********************
```

On executing the program, you will notice that patrons *Das* and *Smith* are the only two people with reduced *newfines*. Das (see screen below), now has to pay a *newfine* of $ 11.11. He was originally scheduled to pay a *fine* of $ 36.50. Patron *Smith* does not pay a fine at all as his old *fine* was $ 2.90.

Patron ID:	250
Patron Name:	Das
Call Number:	600
Fine Due:	$11.11

11
DATABASE 2 (DB2)

DATABASE 2, better known as DB2, is an IBM product based on their research prototype System R. It is a relational database management system, and therefore, has all the advantages of relational database models. As expected, it provides for data definition, data manipulation, integrity control, concurrency control, and recovery.

IBM has also announced a new DB2 release that features a distributed data capability. DB2 Version 2 Release 2 also allows one DB2 database to communicate with another, giving customers access to information stored in multiple larger systems within their organization. The above capability will be offered across all computing environments as part of IBM's plan to provide distributed data capability through its Systems Application Architecture (SAA). DB2 interfaces very well with IBM's other major database system based on the hierarchical model) called IMS. Currently some large organizations use IMS as their main database system for high volume processing and DB2 as their secondary database system for applications, where ease of use is desirable.

11.1 DB2 Utilities and Related Products

In addition to the facilities provided by SQL, such as data definition, manipulation, and control, several other DB2 utilities are available. There is a utility program to copy part of a table to another (or the whole table, if desired) and a load utility to transfer a sequential file into a DB2 table. Dual-logging capability is supported, and recovery of a damaged table using either a backup copy or a log file is also available. The following members of the DB2 product family are also accessible from DB2:

- *Application Generator.* CSP (Cross System Product) — Builds applications and screens with DB2 data; uses prompts and *fill-in-the-blanks.*

- *Interactive Facility.* DB2I (DB2 Interactive) — Consists of associated screens and panels and allows execution of various DB2 operations: prepare and run application programs, submit commands, run utilities. Along with SPUFI (SQL Processor using File Input) it allows the DP user to execute SQL statements interactively.

- *Performance Management.* DB2PM — Gathers statistics on accounting and performance data. Helpful for tuning.

- *Query Management and Reporting:* QMF (Query Management Facility) — User-friendly facility for building reports and querying files. Similar to DB2I (SPUFI), but QMF (QBE) is used by the end user whereas DB2I (SPUFI) is used by DP professionals.

- *Host Access:* DXT (Data Extract) — Extracts data from DL/I, SQL/DS, and DB2 databases.

- *PC Access:* HDBV (Host Data Base View) — Downloads the appropriate data from DB2 and formats it for use on the IBM-PC (in an application). Popular spreadsheet and database formats are supported.

- *Business Planning and Decision Support.* AS (Application System) — Helps with project planning, statistical analysis, text processing, and financial planning.

- *Graphics.* QMFASF (Application Support Facility) — Converts queries and data into graphics.

- *Systems Management:* DBRAD (Relational Application Directory) — Information on DB2 tables, concurrent access and programming aids.

- *Database Edit and Update.* DBEDIT — Allows easy edits and updates to DB2 tables. Avoids need to use SQL.

11.2 Operating Environment

Access to DB2 database is permitted from within IMS, CICS, and TSO. The data stored in DB2 can be accessed concurrently by application programs written in COBOL, FORTRAN, PL/I, or Assembly, using either IMS/VS, CICS, or TSO/ISPF. Figure 11.1 illustrates the relationship of DB2 in the IBM Operating Environment. We notice that DB2 tables are shared by IMS, CICS, and TSO interactive or embedded applications. Products such as CSP, QMF, and DXT can be used to connect the above three subsystems.

Figure 11.1 Operating Environment

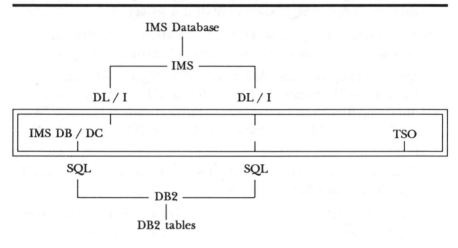

11.3 Using DB2 SQL

In this section we cover various aspects of DB2 such as data definition, data types, manipulation, and views. As indicated earlier, all SQL statements can be executed interactively through SPUFI or QMF, or through embedded statements in application programs.

11.3.1   Data definition

Data definition commands in DB2 are similar to those introduced in Part A. They include **CREATE** and **DROP** commands for tables, views and indexes, and an **ALTER** command for tables. NULLs are supported in DB2. DB2 tables can have up to 64 gigabytes each, and they can be divided into partitions that can be loaded, reorganized and recovered individually (see Table 9.1).

11.3.2   Data types

The following data types are available:

INTEGER   Signed numbers not including decimals.

DECIMAL   Digits in the format *(p,s)* where *p* represents the precision and *s* the scale.

FLOATING   Can be single- or double-precision. Single-precision real numbers are approximated to 32 bits; double-precision real numbers are approximated to 64 bits.

CHARACTER   Can be of *fixed* or *varying* length. An example for *varying length* would be the *title* column of the BOOK table; an example for *fixed* length would be the *user_id* column (here assumed non-numeric). These are called **VARCHAR/LONGCHAR** and **CHAR** respectively.

DATE   Allows specification of data type. It can be converted to various formats on input or output.

> **TIME** Allows specification and manipulation of **TIME** fields.

11.3.3 Data manipulation

DB2 supports the four data manipulation statements discussed in part A: **SELECT, INSERT, UPDATE,** and **DELETE.** The various examples presented in part A can be executed readily in DB2 with the exception of the following SQL statements: **OUTER JOIN, INTERSECT,** and **MINUS.** The latest release support *referential integrity*.

The **UNION** operator is less rigid in DB2 Release 3. For example, consider the following query:

> **SELECT** a, b
> **FROM** TABLE 1
> **UNION**
> **SELECT** c, d
> **FROM** TABLE 2;

Here the columns *a, b, c* and *d* do not have to be exactly of the same data type, the same size, or have the same NULL specification. Data types have to be compatible. A **UNION ALL** operator is now available, it does not sort data and does not eliminate duplicates; therefore, it is faster than **UNION.**

The following synonyms have been added in DB2 to align it more closely with the ANS SQL Standard.

KEYWORD	SYNONYM
ANY	SOME
INTEGER	INT
DECIMAL	DEC
CHAR	CHARACTER

11.3.4 Views

Views provide automatic security by hiding data; moreover, they allow the user to focus on relevant data. With DB2, views can involve one or more tables. **JOIN**s and built-in functions can be used. However, **UNION** and **ORDER BY** cannot be used. DB2 allows you to define views on top of existing views.

11.4 DB2 Administration

In this section we describe the DB2 catalog, links, table spaces, storage groups, logging and recovery.

Catalog

The DB2 catalog keeps track of all system objects such as the base tables, indexes, views, databases, and access privileges. The catalog itself is defined as tables and can be used for querying. The catalog tables are updated by DB2 automatically during execution of SQL DDL statements. All columns in the catalog tables are specified as **NOT NULL**. All authorized users can browse through the catalog tables; however, it is not possible to update the catalog information manually (by the user). This prevents accidental loss of system data. Some important DB2 catalog tables are:

SYSCOLUMNS   Contains a row for every column of every table in the entire system. Provides information such as column name, column type, and table name.

SYSTABLES   Contains a row for every base table and provides information such as table creator, number of columns in the table, and date created.

SYSINDEXES   Each row provides the name of an index and the indexed table.

Refer to section 7.4 for more information on SYSTABLES. The SYSCOLUMNS table and SYSTABAUTH table are described next.

SYSCOLUMNS

The table call SYSCOLUMNS contains a list of all columns defined in the database. The columns in SYSCOLUMNS itself include: *name, tabname, tbcreator, colno, coltype, length, scale, nulls, updates, remarks, keyseq, foreignkey.*

Some of the attributes of SYSIBM.SYSCOLUMNS are described below:

name Column name

tbname Name of the table or view that contains the column

tbcreator Name of the person who created the table

coltype Describes the datatype, **INTEGER, CHAR, DATE,** . . .

nulls Can be Y or N. Yes: the column can contain a null value; No: the column cannot contain a null value

updates The value can be Y or N

keyseq Indicates the numerical place of the column within a primary key. 0 means it is not part of a primary key

foreignkey Can be Y or N. Indicates if the column is part of a foreign key

The following query would extract useful information from the table SYSCOLUMNS:

SELECT name, tbname, colno, coltype, length, nulls, remarks
FROM SYSIBM.SYSCOLUMNS
WHERE tbcreator = 'Carlson';

The above query can be qualified further if required:

SELECT name
FROM SYSIBM.SYSCOLUMNS
WHERE tbname = 'BOOK';
AND tbcreator = 'Carlson';

Result: **name**

    call_no
    title
    subject

SYSTABAUTH

This table records the privileges held by users on tables or views. The columns of this table are: *grantor, grantee, granteetype, dbname, tcreator, authhowgot, dategranted, timegranted, alterauth, deleteauth, indexauth, updateauth*.

Some of the attributes of SYSIBM.SYSTABAUTH are described below:

grantor: Authorization ID of the user who granted the privileges

grantee: ID of the user who received the privilege

dategranted: Date the privileges were granted

alterauth: Indicates whether or not the grantee can alter the table

deleteauth: Indicates whether or not the grantee can delete rows

indexauth: Indicates whether or not the grantee can index the table

updateauth: Indicates whether or not the grantee can update rows of the table or view

authhowgot: Indicates how the privileges were received, for example

        S indicates from the System Administrator

        D indicates from the Database Administrator

In the four columns, *alterauth, deleteauth, indexauth,* and *updateauth,* there can be three possible values:

- a *blank* indicating that the privilege is not held,
- **G** indicating that privilege is held with **GRANT OPTION**,
- or **Y** indicating that privilege is held without **GRANT** option.

Consider the following example which provides information on who granted authority to whom:

> **SELECT** grantor, grantee
> **FROM** SYSIBM.SYSTABAUTH
> **WHERE** tbcreator = 'Carlson';

Result:	name	grantor	grantee
	BOOK	Carlson	Smith
	BOOK	Smith	Nordin

Links in DB2 CATALOG

An item called *links* is contained in the DB2 catalog. It connects two tables, the *parent table* and the *child table.* For example, SYSIBM.SYSDATABASE is a *parent* and SYSIBM.SYSDBAUTH is the *child.* The former records the existence of databases and the latter keeps track of the privileges held by different users over the database. SYSDBAUTH is the *child* because it cannot exist unless a database exists. Any table can be both a parent and a child.

Storage groups

A *table space* or collection of *table spaces* are allocated to a DB2 database. Only tables from the same database are placed in the same table space (see figure 11.2). Table spaces can be identified with *storage groups.* Storage groups consist of a set of disk volumes. If the tables need more storage, DB2 will automatically allocate more space within a storage group.

The table space can further be partitioned on the basis of *ranges*. For examples in the BOOK table, we can partition the table space by subject. The advantage with this strategy is that these independent partitions can be recovered individually. Moreover, they can also be reorganized independently. The above information is also conveyed in figure 11.2.

Figure 11.2 Storage Groups

LIBRARY DATABASE	
Table Space One	
LOAN table	. . . . . . storage group 1
PATRON table	. . . . . storage group 2
Table Space Two	
Book table — partition one	. . . . . storage group 2
BOOK table — partition two	. . . . . . storage group 3
BOOK table — partition three	. . . . . storage group 4
Table Space N . .	. . . . . storage group 4

Logging and recovery

Logging and recovery are important aspects of any database system; DB2 is no exception. Let us look at the various DB2 utilities and procedures involved in this process. A table space is the recoverable unit in DB2, for example Table_Space_One in figure 11.2. A complete image copy of the table space is made initially. All changes made to the table space are recorded by DB2 in a *log*. A log keeps track of all the changes made since the last image copy was made. In the event that a failure does occur, we reapply all the changes recorded in the log onto the table space. This is known as *forward recovery*.

The utilities provided to enable logging and recovery are:

- Image Copy Utility: Copies the table space.
- Log: Records the changes to the image copy in the log.
- Recovery Utility: Reapplies all changes recorded in the log to rebuild the table space.

Often *incremental-image* copies have to be made, as making full-image copies can be time-consuming. In this case, the incremental changes can merge with the image copy to construct the *full image copy*. DB2 will maintain two sets of active and two sets of archive logs if required (dual-logging). This is useful; if a log fails, DB2 will ensure that the recovery operation is not jeopardized.

11.5 Developing DB2 Applications

In this section we describe the use of SQL statements to retrieve and manipulate data using an application program. DB2I panels are used to describe this, since DB2I is easiest and is commonly used by application programmers. The following sequence of steps illustrates the procedure for developing DB2 applications. (It synchronizes with the primary menu items of the DB2I — see screen on next page.)

a. Obtain the DB2I menu using ISPF (Interactive System Productivity Facility) at the terminal.

b. A screen describing the following options appears:

DB2I Primary Option Menu

Select one of the following DB2 functions and press *enter*

1. SPUFI
2. DCLGEN
3. PROGRAM PREPARATION
4. PRECOMPILE

5. BIND/REBIND/FREE
6. RUN
7. DB2 COMMANDS
8. UTILITIES
D. DB2I DEFAULTS
X. EXIT

---

c. Select option number 1, SPUFI. It is used to develop interactive procedures and can be used to test SQL statements that we plan to embed in the application program.

d. Select option number 2. DCLGEN is used to generate source language *declarations. DCLGEN saves time as it eliminates the need to write declare statements manually.* it is used by COBOL or PL/I programmers to generate a complete SQL description of a table for inclusion in a program. The declarations are put in a library.

e. The application program is written next (by selecting option number 3) using a host language such as COBOL or PL/I. The program can be written for any of three environments, IMS/VS BMP (Batch Message Processing), MPP (Message Processing Program), or CICS program. The declarations placed in the library earlier can now be retrieved by using **SQL INCLUDE** statements. The application program is written using the Embedded SQL statements tested earlier. (Consult the COBOL and PL/I examples in chapter 8 for detailed information).

f. The application program is precompiled using option number 4. The SQL statements are flagged during precompilation as comment statements, and necessary code to interact with DB2 is inserted. Three outputs result here:

- The modified application program (with inserted code)

- A listing to debug SQL statements in the program.

- The DBRM (Data Base Request Module) which is input to the *bind* process

g. Binding is done next (option number 5). It involves converting the DBRM into an *application plan.* This plan tells DB2 where the data is, how to access it, and what to do with it. Once a bind is successfully created it automatically *rebinds* whenever changes occur to the data definition or indexes, to recreate a new application plan.

h. Finally, the program is compiled, linked and run (this is invoked in a "Secondary Option Menu" and is not displayed here).

Table 11.1 DB2 and SQL Limits

The limitations and restrictions imposed by DB2 are described below:

Maximum columns in a table or view:	300 or less.
Longest row of a table:	4K for 4K pages, 32K for 32K pages.
Largest integer value:	2147483647
Smallest integer value:	–2147483648
Largest small integer value:	32767
Smallest small integer value:	–32768
Largest float value:	7.2E+75
Smallest float value:	–7.2E-75
Largest decimal value:	999999999999999
Smallest decimal value:	–999999999999999
Maximum tables selected:	15 or less (depending on complexity).
Longest SQL statement:	32K
Maximum # of columns in an index key:	16
maximum indexes on a table:	Limited by system storage
Largest table space:	64 gigabytes
Longest synonym *(name of a column, table, or index):*	18 bytes

---

Appendixes

Appendix A
International Bank

The background material to questions assigned at the end of each chapter is presented here.

International Bank has a Computer Division which looks after the information and application systems for the entire organization. They have recently purchased an SQL-based relational database system, and are interested in developing new applications using SQL.

Sample Application Tables

The following application tables have been identified.

- CUSTOMER Table
- ACCOUNT Table
- TRANSACTIONS Table

CUSTOMER table

This table lists all the customers of International Bank. The customers include both businesses and individuals. The format and content of the table is described below.

Column Name	Description
id	identifies the customer uniquely
name	name of individuals or businesses
credit_rating	excellent, good, poor, bad
address	address of the business/individual

ACCOUNT table

The account table keeps track of the various accounts of each customer. A customer may have more than one type of account. Such information is stored in the account table. Also the credit limit of each account is indicated here. Business accounts have credit limits, individual accounts do not and therefore have a value of zero.

Column Name	Description
id	identifies the business uniquely
account-no	business account number
current_bal	current balance of the account
credit_limit	describes the maximum credit available

TRANSACTION table

A check or a deposit is considered to be a transaction. Checks are identified by a negative value. Any number with a minus sign is a check and it decreases the current balance. Deposits can be identified in the transaction column by a positive value. They increase the current balance.

Column Name	Description
account_no	savings account number
date	date of transaction
amount	deposits/checks written

Table Relationship for Sample Application

The customer table is connected to the account table via the common column *id*, and the account table in turn is connected to the transactions table through the *account_no* column.

Sample Records

Sample records for the above database are presented below:

CUSTOMER

id	name	credit_rating	address
100	zappa	good	101 apple ave, toronto
101	baker	poor	202-100 gateway, atlanta
102	higgins	excellent	101 main st, winnipeg
103	kent	excellent	555 dallas ave, austin
104	dattani	excellent	6549 elwell st, vancouver
105	burns	poor	100-100 nowhere st, new york
106	mcdonald	good	50 bay st, melbourne
107	mike	poor	100 jolly ave, miami
108	sam	good	155-300 height ave, edmonton
109	jones	good	850-555 royal ave, london

ACCOUNT

id	account_no	current_bal	credit_limit
100	01111	4000	10000
101	20304	−5000	0
102	45671	10000	3000
103	12345	−55	1000
104	10000	90000	10000
105	00034	−1200	0
106	89000	7576	2000
107	22200	2553	0
108	10101	1312	300
109	50001	10061	5000

TRANSACTION

account_no	date	amount
01111	10-sep-89	12000
01111	02-jan-90	725
12345	12-dec-89	10000
10000	22-jun-90	300
00034	22-jul-90	1200
22200	05-aug-89	101
01111	03-aug-89	90000

Appendix B
SQL Command Language Syntax

Key to Syntax and Notation

brackets [ ]	Item within brackets is optional
braces { I }	Enter one of the items separated by the I
elipses . . .	Preceding items may be repeated several times.
parenthesis (,)	Parenthesis and commas should be typed.
underline __	Default value.
expr	*expr* refers to any expression consisting of column names and constants separated by arithmetic operation (+ , − , / and *).

Data Definition Commands

ALTER TABLE TABLE {**ADD** I **MODIFY**} (column [**NULL** I **NOT NULL**], . . .);

CREATE [**UNIQUE**] **INDEX** name
   ON TABLE (column [**ASC** I **DESC**], column [**ASC** I **DESC**], . . .);

CREATE TABLE TABLE (column [**NOT NULL**], . . .);

CREATE TABLE TABLE [(COLUMN [**NOT NULL**], . . .)]
   [**AS** query];

CREATE VIEW NAME [(alias,alias, . . .)] **AS** query
   [**WITH CHECK OPTION**];

DROP {**INDEX** INDEX [**ON** TABLE] I **TABLE** TABLE I **VIEW** VIEW};

DATA Manipulation and Retrieval Commands

DELETE FROM TABLE [WHERE condition];

INSERT INTO TABLE [(column, column, . . .)]
  {VALUES (value, value, . . .) | query];

SELECT [ALL | DISTINCT] {[TABLE] * | expr, expr, . . .}
  FROM TABLE [alias], TABLE [alias], . . .
  [WHERE condition]
  [GROUP BY expr, expr, . . .] [HAVING condition]
  [{UNION | INTERSECT | MINUS} SELECT . . .]
  [ORDER BY {expr | position} [ASC | DESC], {expr | position} [ASC | DESC] . . .};

> Note: **ORDER BY** and **FOR UPDATE OF** clauses are valid only in **SELECT**
> commands, not in subqueries.

UPDATE TABLE [ALIAS]
  SET column = expr, column = expr, . . .
  [WHERE condition];

Operators Used in SQL Commands

Value operators

Operator	Function
( )	Overrides normal operator precedence rules
+ −	Prefix sign for a number expression
* /	Multiplication & Division
+ −	Addition & Subtraction
			Character concatenation

Logical operators

Operator	Function
( )	Overrides normal operator precedence rules.
=	Test for equality.
! = ^ = l < >	Test for inequality.
> l >= l < l <=	Greater than, greater than or equal to, less than, less than or equal to.
NOT IN	Not equal to any member of; also equivalent to ' ! =ALL ' .
IN	Equal to any member of; equivalent to ' = ANY ' .
ANY	Compares a value to each value returned by a list or subquery.
ALL	Compares a value to every value returned by a list or subquery.
BETWEEN x and y	Greater than or equal to x, and less than or equal to y.
EXISTS	"True" if a subquery returned at least one row.
LIKE	Matches following pattern: ' % ' matches any sequence of characters; and ' _ ' matches any single character.
IS NULL	Column value is null
NOT	Reverses a logical expression's result; the following operators can be used: **NOT BETWEEN, NOT EXISTS, NOT LIKE, NOT NULL**
AND	Combines logical expressions to be True if both are True
OR	Combines logical expressions to be True if either is True

Query expression operators

UNION Combines queries to return all distinct rows returned by either one individually

INTERSECT Combines queries to return all distinct rows returned by both individually

MINUS Combines queries to return all distinct rows returned by first but not the second.

GROUP FUNCTIONS

AVG([DISTINCT] expr) Average value of expr. Null values ignored.

COUNT(DISTINCT expr | *) Counts instances (ignoring nulls). **COUNT(*)** docs not ignore nulls.

MAX([DISTINCT] expr) Maximum value of expression. Null values ignored.

MIN([DISTINCT] expr) Minimum value of expression. Null values ignored.

SUM([DISTINCT] expr) Sum of values. Null values ignored.

MISCELLANEOUS COMMANDS

Recovery

ROLLBACK [WORK];
COMMIT [WORK];

Security and access control commands

GRANT [privilege, privilege, . . . | **ALL** }
ON TABLE
TO { user, user, . . . | **PUBLIC** }
[**WITH GRANT OPTION**];

REVOKE { privilege | **ALL** } **ON** TABLE
FROM {user,user, . . . | **PUBLIC** };

Note: Privilege is one of:
SELECT | **INSERT** | **DELETE** | **UPDATE** [(column-list)]

RESERVED WORDS

(Cannot be used as Identifiers)

ALL	**DEC**
AND	**DECIMAL**
ANY	**DECLARE**
AS	**DELETE**
ASC	**DESC**
AUTHORIZATION	**DISTINCT**
AVG	**DOUBLE**
BEGIN	**END**
BETWEEN	**ESCAPE**
BY	**EXEC**
CHAR	**EXISTS**
CHARACTER	**FETCH**
CHECK	**FLOAT**
CLOSE	**FOR**
COBOL	**FORTRAN**
COMMIT	**FOUND**
CONTINUE	**FROM**
COUNT	**GO**
CREATE	**GOTO**
CURRENT	**GRANT**
CURSOR	**GROUP**

HAVING
IN
INDICATOR
INSERT
INT
INTEGER
INTO
IS
LANGUAGE
LIKE
MAX
MIN
MODULE
NOT
NULL
NUMERIC
OF
ON
OPEN
OPTION
OR
ORDER
PASCAL
PLI
PRECISION
PRIVILEGES

PUBLIC
REAL
ROLLBACK
SCHEMA
SECTION
SELECT
SET
SMALLINT
SOME
SQL
SQLCODE
SQLERROR
SUM
TABLE
TO
UNION
UNIQUE
UPDATE
USER
VALUES
VIEW
WHENEVER
WHERE
WITH
WORK

Answers to Exercises

Answers to selected odd-numbered exercises

Chapter 2

2.1 (a) **CREATE TABLE** CUSTOMER (
        id   **INTEGER NOT NULL,**
        name   **CHARACTER**(15) **NOT NULL,**
        credit_rating **CHARACTER**(9),
        address   **CHARACTER**(30));

2.5 **DROP TABLE** TRANSACTION;

Chapter 3

3.3 **SELECT** id, credit_limit
    FROM ACCOUNT;

3.5 **SELECT** name
    FROM CUSTOMER c, ACCOUNT a
    WHERE c.id = a.id
    AND a.credit_limit > = 5000;

3.7 **SELECT** id, current_bal
    FROM ACCOUNT
    WHERE id = 100;

3.9 **SELECT DISTINCT**(c.name)
   FROM CUSTOMER c, ACCOUNT a, TRANSACTION t
   WHERE c.id = a.id
       AND a.account_no = t.account_no
       AND t.amount > = 1000;

3.11 **SELECT DISTINCT**(address)
    FROM CUSTOMER;

3.13 **SELECT** id
    FROM ACCOUNT
    WHERE current_bal = (**SELECT MAX**(current_bal)
                  FROM ACCOUNT);

3.15 **SELECT** a.id, t.account_no, t.t_date, t.amount
    FROM ACCOUNT a, TRANSACTION t
    WHERE a.account_no = t.account_no
       AND a.id **IN** (100, 103, 104, 108)
    ORDER BY a.id;

3.17 **SELECT** name
    FROM CUSTOMER
    ORDER BY name;

3.19 **SELECT COUNT(*)**
    FROM CUSTOMER
    WHERE credit_rating = 'excellent';

3.21 **SELECT** c.id, c.name, a.current_bal
    FROM CUSTOMER c, ACCOUNT a
    WHERE c.id = a.id;

3.23 **SELECT** c.name
    FROM CUSTOMER c, ACCOUNT a
    WHERE c.id = a.id
       AND a.current_bal > 4000;

3.25 **SELECT** c.name, a.id, t.account_no, t.t_date, t.amount
FROM CUSTOMER c, ACCOUNT a, TRANSACTION t
WHERE c.id = a.id
   AND a.account_no = t.account_no;

3.27 **SELECT** account_no
FROM ACCOUNT
WHERE account_no **NOT IN** (**SELECT DISTINCT**(account_no)
                        FROM TRANSACTION)
ORDER BY account_no;

Note: can also be accomplished by using the minus operator,
(account – transaction)

Chapter 4

4.1 **UPDATE** CUSTOMERS
SET credit_rating = 'Good'
WHERE credit_rating = 'V.Good';

4.5 **UPDATE** ACCOUNT
SET current_bal = (**SELECT SUM**(amount)
                FROM TRANSACTION
                WHERE account_no = 01111)
WHERE account_no = 01111;

Further Reading

1. Astrahan, M. M., and R. A. Lorie. "SEQUEL-XRM: A Relational System." Proc. of the Pacific Regional Conference, San Francisco, April 1975.

2. Astrahan, M. M., et al. "System R: Relational Approach to Database Management." *ACM Transactions on Database Systems* 1, no. 2 (June 1976).

3. Chamberlin, D. D., and R. F. Boyce. "Sequel: A Structured English Query Language." Proc. of the ACM SIGMOD Workshop on Data Description, Access, and Control, Ann Arbor, May 1974.

4. Chamberlin, D. C. "A Summary of User Experience with the SQL Data Sublanguage." Proc. of the International Conference on Databases, Aberdeen, Scotland, July 1980.

5. Chamberlin, D. D. et al. "A History and Evaluation of System R." *Communications of the ACM* 24, no. 10 (October 1981).

6. *Database Language SQL.* American National Standards Institute DOC. ANSI X3.135, 1986.

7. *Database Language SQL Addendum-2.* American National Standards Institute Document X3H2-86-61, May, 1986.

8. Date, C. J., and C. J. White. *A Guide to DB2.* Addison-Wesley, 1988.

9. Date, C.J. *A Guide to the SQL Standard.* Addison-Wesley, 1987.

10. _____. *A Guide to Ingres.* Addison-Wesley, 1987.

11. Dimmick, S. *ORACLE Database Administrator's Guide.* Belmont, CA, ORACLE, 1986.

12. Sachs, J. *SQL*Plus User's Guide.* Belmont, CA, ORACLE, 1986.

Index